ns

MOPSA THE F[
BY
Jean Ingelow

MOPSA THE FAIRY

Published by Mythik Press

New York City, NY

First published circa 1897

Copyright © Mythik Press, 2015

All rights reserved

Except in the United States of America, this book is sold subject to the condition that it shall not, by way of trade or otherwise, be lent, re-sold, hired out, or otherwise circulated without the publisher's prior consent in any form of binding or cover other than that in which it is published and without a similar condition including this condition being imposed on the subsequent purchaser.

ABOUT MYTHIK PRESS

From the moment people first began practicing rituals, they have been creating folk tales and legends to celebrate their past and create a unique cultural identity. **Mythik Press** carries these legacies forward by publishing the greatest stories ever concocted, from King Arthur to the fairy tales of the Brothers Grimm.

CHAPTER I. ABOVE THE CLOUDS.

"And can this be my own world? 'Tis all gold and snow, Save where scarlet waves are hurled Down yon gulf below." "'Tis thy world, 'tis my world, City, mead, and shore, For he that hath his own world Hath many worlds more."

A boy, whom I knew very well, was once going through a meadow, which was full of buttercups. The nurse and his baby sister were with him; and when they got to an old hawthorn, which grew in the hedge and was covered with blossom, they all sat down in its shade, and the nurse took out three slices of plum-cake, gave 2 one to each of the children, and kept one for herself.

While the boy was eating, he observed that this hedge was very high and thick, and that there was a great hollow in the trunk of the old thorn-tree, and he heard a twittering, as if there was a nest somewhere inside; so he thrust his head in, twisted himself round, and looked up.

It was a very great thorn-tree, and the hollow was so large that two or three boys could have stood upright in it; and when he got used to the dim light in that brown, still place, he saw that a good way above his head there was a nest,—rather a curious one, too, for it was as large as a pair of blackbirds would have built,—and yet it was made of fine white wool and delicate bits of moss; in short, it was like a goldfinch's nest magnified three times.

Just then he thought he heard some little voices cry, "Jack! Jack!" His baby sister was asleep, and the nurse was reading a story-book, so it could not have been either of them who called. "I 3 must get in here," said the boy. "I wish this hole was larger." So he began to wriggle and twist himself through, and just as he pulled in his last foot, he looked up, and three heads which had been peeping over the edge of the nest suddenly popped down again.

"Those heads had no beaks, I am sure," said Jack, and he stood on tiptoe and poked in one of his fingers. "And the things have no feathers," he continued; so, the hollow being rather rugged, he managed to climb up and look in.

His eyes were not used yet to the dim light; but he was sure those things were not birds,—no. He poked them, and they took no notice; but when he snatched one of them out of the nest, it gave a loud squeak, and said, "O don't, Jack!" as plainly as possible, upon which he was so frightened that he lost his footing, dropped the thing, and slipped down himself. Luckily, he was not hurt, nor the thing either; he could see it quite plainly now: it was creeping about like 4 rather an old baby, and had on a little frock and pinafore.

"It's a fairy!" exclaimed Jack to himself. "How curious! and this must be a fairy's nest. Oh, how angry the old mother will be if this little thing creeps away and gets out of the hole!" So he looked down. "Oh, the hole is on the other side," he said; and he turned round, but the hole was not on the other side; it was not on any side; it must have closed up all on a sudden, while he was looking into the nest, for, look whichever way he would, there was no hole at all, excepting a very little one high up over the nest, which let in a very small sunbeam.

Jack was very much astonished, but he went on eating his cake, and was so delighted to see the young fairy climb up the side of the hollow and scramble again into her nest, that he laughed heartily; upon which all the nestlings popped up their heads, and, showing their pretty white teeth, pointed at the slice of cake.

"Well," said Jack, "I may have to stay inside 5 here for a long time, and I have nothing to eat but this cake; however, your mouths are very small, so you shall have a piece;" and he broke off a small piece, and put it into the nest, climbing up to see them eat it.

These young fairies were a long time dividing and munching the cake, and before they had finished, it began to be rather dark, for a black cloud came over and covered the little sunbeam. At the same time the wind rose, and rocked the boughs, and made the old tree creak and tremble. Then there was thunder and rain, and the little fairies were so frightened that they got out of the nest and crept into Jack's pockets. One got into each waistcoat pocket, and the other two were very comfortable, for he took out his handkerchief and made room for them in the pocket of his jacket.

It got darker and darker, till at last Jack could only just see the hole, and it seemed to be a very long way off. Every time he looked at it, it was farther off, and at last he saw a thin crescent moon shining through it.

"I am sure it cannot be night yet," he said; and he took out one of the fattest of the young fairies, and held it up towards the hole.

"Look at that," said he; "what is to be done now? the hole is so far off that it's night up there, and down here I haven't done eating my lunch."

"Well," answered the young fairy, "then why don't you whistle?"

Jack was surprised to hear her speak in this sensible manner, and in the light of the moon he looked at her very attentively.

"When first I saw you in the nest," said he, "you had a pinafore on, and now you have a smart little apron, with lace round it."

"That is because I am much older now," said the fairy; "we never take such a long time to grow up as you do."

"But your pinafore?" said Jack.

"Turned into an apron, of course," replied the fairy, "just as your velvet jacket will turn into a tail-coat when you are old enough."

"It won't," said Jack.

"Yes it will," answered the fairy, with an air of superior wisdom. "Don't argue with me; I am older now than you are,—nearly grown up, in fact. Put me into your pocket again, and whistle as loudly as you can."

Jack laughed, put her in, and pulled out another. "Worse and worse," he said; "why, this was a boy fairy, and now he has a mustache and a sword, and looks as fierce as possible!"

"I think I heard my sister tell you to whistle?" said this fairy, very sternly.

"Yes, she did," said Jack. "Well, I suppose I had better do it." So he whistled very loudly indeed.

"Why did you leave off so soon?" said another of them, peeping out.

"Why, if you wish to know," answered Jack, "it was because I thought something took hold of my legs."

"Ridiculous child!" cried the last of the four, 8 "how do you think you are ever to get out, if she doesn't take hold of your legs?"

Jack thought he would rather have done a long-division sum than have been obliged to whistle; but he could not help doing it when they told him, and he felt something take hold of his legs again, and then give him a jerk, which hoisted him on to its back, where he sat astride, and wondered whether the thing was a pony; but it was not, for he presently observed that it had a very slender neck, and then that it was covered with feathers. It was a large bird, and he presently found that they were rising towards the hole, which had become so very far off, and in a few minutes she dashed through the hole, with Jack on her back and all the fairies in his pockets.

It was so dark that he could see nothing, and he twined his arms round the bird's neck, to hold on, upon which this agreeable fowl told him not to be afraid, and said she hoped he was comfortable.

"I should be more comfortable," replied Jack, "if I knew how I could get home again. I don't wish to go home just yet, for I want to see where we are flying to, but papa and mamma will be frightened if I never do."

"Oh no," replied the albatross (for she was an albatross), "you need not be at all afraid about that. When boys go to Fairyland, their parents never are uneasy about them."

"Really?" exclaimed Jack.

"Quite true," replied the albatross.

"And so we are going to Fairyland?" exclaimed Jack; "how delightful!"

"Yes," said the albatross; "the back way, mind; we are only going the back way. You could go in two minutes by the usual route; but these young fairies want to go before they are summoned, and therefore you and I are taking them." And she continued to fly on in the dark sky for a very long time.

"They seem to be all fast asleep," said Jack.

"Perhaps they will sleep till we come to the 10 wonderful river," replied the albatross; and just then she flew with a great bump against something that met her in the air.

"What craft is this that hangs out no light?" said a gruff voice.

"I might ask the same question of you," answered the albatross, sullenly.

"I'm only a poor Will-o'-the-wisp," replied the voice, "and you know very well that I have but a lantern to show." Thereupon a lantern became visible, and Jack saw by the light of it a man, who looked old and tired, and he was so transparent that you could see through him, lantern and all.

"I hope I have not hurt you, William," said the albatross; "I will light up immediately. Good-night."

"Good-night," answered the Will-o'-the-wisp. "I am going down as fast as I can; the storm blew me up, and I am never easy excepting in my native swamps."

Jack might have taken more notice of Will, 11 if the albatross had not begun to light up. She did it in this way. First, one of her eyes began to gleam with a beautiful green light, which cast its rays far and near, and then, when it was as bright as a lamp, the other eye began to shine, and the light of that eye was red. In short, she was lighted up just like a vessel at sea.

Jack was so happy that he hardly knew which to look at first, there really were so many remarkable things.

"They snore," said the albatross, "they are very fast asleep, and before they wake I should like to talk to you a little."

She meant that the fairies snored, and so they did, in Jack's pockets.

"My name," continued the albatross, "is Jenny. Do you think you shall remember that? because, when you are in Fairyland and want some one to take you home again, and call 'Jenny,' I shall be able to come to you; and I shall come with pleasure, for I like boys better than fairies."

"Thank you," said Jack. "Oh yes, I shall 12 remember your name, it is such a very easy one."

"If it is in the night that you want me, just look up," continued the albatross, "and you will see a green and a red spark moving in the air; you will then call Jenny, and I will come; but remember that I cannot come unless you do call me."

"Very well," said Jack; but he was not attending, because there was so much to be seen.

In the first place, all the stars excepting a few large ones were gone, and they looked frightened; and as it got lighter, one after the other seemed to give a little start in the blue sky and go out. And then Jack looked down and saw, as he thought, a great country, covered with very jagged snow mountains with astonishingly sharp peaks. Here and there he saw a very deep lake,—at least he thought it was a lake; but while he was admiring the mountains, there came an enormous crack between two of the largest, and he saw the sun 13 come rolling up among them, and it seemed to be almost smothered.

"Why, those are clouds!" exclaimed Jack; "and O how rosy they have all turned! I thought they were mountains."

"Yes, they are clouds," said the albatross; and then they turned gold color; and next they began to plunge and tumble, and every one of the peaks put on a glittering crown; and next they broke themselves to pieces, and began to drift away. In fact, Jack had been out all night, and now it was morning.

CHAPTER II. CAPTAIN JACK.

All this time the albatross kept dropping down and down like a stone, till Jack was quite out of breath, and they fell or flew, whichever you like to call it, straight through one of the great chasms which he had thought were lakes, and he looked down, as he sat on the bird's back, to see what the world is like when you hang a good way above it at sunrise.

It was a very beautiful sight; the sheep and lambs were still fast asleep on the green hills, and 15 the sea-birds were asleep in long rows upon the ledges of the cliffs, with their heads under their wings.

"Are those young fairies awake yet?" asked the albatross.

"As sound asleep as ever," answered Jack; "but, Albatross, is not that the sea which lies under us? You are a sea-bird, I know, but I am not a sea boy, and I cannot live in the water."

"Yes, that is the sea," answered the albatross. "Don't you observe that it is covered with ships?"

"I see boats and vessels," answered Jack, "and all their sails are set, but they cannot sail, because there is no wind."

"The wind never does blow in this great bay," said the bird; "and those ships would all lie there becalmed till they dropped to pieces if one of them was not wanted now and then to go up the wonderful river."

"But how did they come there?" asked Jack.

"Some of them had captains who ill-used their cabin-boys, some were pirate ships, and others 16 were going out on evil errands. The consequence was, that when they chanced to sail within this great bay they got becalmed; the fairies came and picked all the sailors out and threw them into the water; they then took away the flags and pennons to make their best coats of, threw the ship-biscuits and other provisions to the fishes, and set all the sails. Many ships which are supposed by men to have foundered lie becalmed in this quiet sea. Look at those five grand ones with high prows; they are moored close together; they were part of the Spanish Armada: and those open boats with blue sails belonged to the Romans; they sailed with Cæsar when he invaded Britain."

By this time the albatross was hovering about among the vessels, making choice of one to take Jack and the fairies up the wonderful river.

"It must not be a large one," she said, "for the river in some places is very shallow."

Jack would have liked very much to have a fine three-master, all to himself; but then he considered that he did not know anything about sails 17 and rigging; he thought it would be just as well to be contented with whatever the albatross might choose, so he let her set him down in a beautiful little open boat, with a great carved figure-head to it. There he seated himself in great state, and the albatross perched herself on the next bench, and faced him.

"You remember my name?" asked the albatross.

"Oh yes," said Jack; but he was not attending,—he was thinking what a fine thing it was to have such a curious boat all to himself.

"That's well," answered the bird; "then, in the next place, are those fairies awake yet?"

"No, they are not," said Jack; and he took them out of his pockets, and laid them down in a row before the albatross.

"They are certainly asleep," said the bird. "Put them away again, and take great care of them. Mind you don't lose any of them, for I really don't know what will happen if you do. 18 Now I have one thing more to say to you, and that is, are you hungry?"

"Rather," said Jack.

"Then," replied the albatross, "as soon as you feel very hungry, lie down in the bottom of the boat and go to sleep. You will dream that you see before you a roasted fowl, some new potatoes, and an apple-pie. Mind you don't eat too much in your dream, or you will be sorry for it when you wake. That is all. Good-by! I must go."

Jack put his arms round the neck of the bird, and hugged her; then she spread her magnificent wings and sailed slowly away. At first he felt very lonely, but in a few minutes he forgot that, because the little boat began to swim so fast.

She was not sailing, for she had no sail, and he was not rowing, for he had no oars; so I am obliged to call her motion swimming, because I don't know of a better word. In less than a quarter of an hour they passed close under the bows of a splendid three-decker, a seventy-gun ship. The gannets who live in those parts had taken possession 19 of her, and she was so covered with nests that you could not have walked one step on her deck without treading on them. The father birds were aloft in the rigging, or swimming in the warm, green sea, and they made such a clamor when they saw Jack that they nearly woke the fairies,—nearly, but not quite, for the little things turned round in Jack's pockets, and sneezed, and began to snore again.

Then the boat swam past a fine brig. Some sea fairies had just flung her cargo overboard, and were playing at leap-frog on deck. These were not at all like Jack's own fairies; they were about the same height and size as himself, and they had brown faces, and red flannel shirts and red caps on. A large fleet of the pearly nautilus was collected close under the vessel's lee. The little creatures were feasting on what the sea fairies had thrown overboard, and Jack's boat, in its eagerness to get on, went plunging through them so roughly that several were capsized. Upon this 20 the brown sea fairies looked over, and called out angrily, "Boat ahoy!" and the boat stopped.

"Tell that boat of yours to mind what she is about," said the fairy sea-captain to Jack.

Jack touched his hat, and said, "Yes, sir," and then called out to his boat, "You ought to be ashamed of yourself, running down these little live fishing-vessels so carelessly. Go at a more gentle pace."

So it swam more slowly; and Jack, being by this time hungry, curled himself up in the bottom of the boat, and fell asleep.

He dreamt directly about a fowl and some potatoes, and he ate a wing, and then he ate a merry-thought, and then somebody said to him that he had better not eat any more, but he did,—he ate another wing; and presently an apple-pie came, and he ate some of that, and then he ate some more, and then he immediately woke.

"Now that bird told me not to eat too much," said Jack, "and yet I have done it. I never felt 21 so full in my life;" and for more than half an hour he scarcely noticed anything.

At last he lifted up his head, and saw straight before him two great brown cliffs, and between them flowed in the wonderful river. Other rivers flow out, but this river flowed in, and took with it far into the land dolphins, sword-fish, mullet, sun-fish, and many other strange creatures; and that is one reason why it was called the magic river, or the wonderful river.

At first it was rather wide, and Jack was alarmed to see what multitudes of soldiers stood on either side to guard the banks, and prevent any person from landing.

He wondered how he should get the fairies on shore. However, in about an hour the river became much narrower, and then Jack saw that the guards were not real soldiers, but rose-colored flamingoes. There they stood, in long regiments, among the reeds, and never stirred. They are the only foot-soldiers the fairies have in their pay; 22 they are very fierce, and never allow anything but a fairy ship to come up the river.

They guarded the banks for miles and miles, many thousands of them, standing a little way into the water among the flags and rushes; but at last there were no more reeds and no soldier guards, for the stream became narrower, and flowed between such steep rocks that no one could possibly have climbed them.

CHAPTER III. WINDING-UP TIME.

"Wake, baillie, wake! the crafts are out; Wake!" said the knight, "be quick! For high street, bye street, over the town They fight with poker and stick." Said the squire, "A fight so fell was ne'er In all thy bailliewick." What said the old clock in the tower? "Tick, tick, tick!"

"Wake, daughter, wake! the hour draws on; Wake!" quoth the dame, "be quick! The meats are set, the guests are coming, The fiddler waxing his stick." She said, "The bridegroom waiting and waiting To see thy face is sick." What said the new clock in her bower? "Tick, tick, tick!"

Jack looked at these hot, brown rocks, first on the left bank and then on the right, till he was quite tired; but at last the shore on the right bank 24 became flat, and he saw a beautiful little bay, where the water was still, and where grass grew down to the brink.

He was so much pleased at this change, that he cried out hastily, "Oh how I wish my boat would swim into that bay and let me land!" He had no sooner spoken than the boat altered her course, as if somebody had been steering her, and began to make for the bay as fast as she could go.

"How odd!" thought Jack. "I wonder whether I ought to have spoken; for the boat certainly did not intend to come into this bay. However, I think I will let her alone now, for I certainly do wish very much to land here."

As they drew towards the strand, the water got so shallow that you could see crabs and lobsters walking about at the bottom. At last the boat's keel grated on the pebbles; and just as Jack began to think of jumping on shore, he saw two little old women approaching, and gently driving a white horse before them.

The horse had panniers, one on each side; and 25 when his feet were in the water he stood still; and Jack said to one of the old women,—"Will you be so kind as to tell me whether this is Fairyland?"

"What does he say?" asked one old woman of the other.

"I asked if this was Fairyland?" repeated Jack, for he thought the first old woman might have been deaf. She was very handsomely dressed in a red satin gown, and did not look in the least like a washer-woman, though it afterwards appeared that she was one.

"He says, 'Is this Fairyland?'" she replied; and the other, who had a blue satin cloak, answered, "Oh, does he?" and then they began to empty the panniers of many small blue, and pink, and scarlet shirts, and coats, and stockings; and when they had made them into two little heaps they knelt down and began to wash them in the river, taking no notice of him whatever.

Jack stared at them. They were not much taller than himself, and they were not taking the slightest 26 care of their handsome clothes; then he looked at the old white horse, who was hanging his head over the lovely clear water with a very discontented air.

At last the blue washer-woman said, "I shall leave off now; I've got a pain in my works."

"Do," said the other. "We'll go home and have a cup of tea." Then she glanced at Jack, who was still sitting in the boat, and said, "Can you strike?"

"I can if I choose," replied Jack, a little astonished at this speech. And the red and blue washer-women wrung out the clothes, put them again into the panniers, and taking the old horse by the bridle, began gently to lead him away.

"I have a great mind to land," thought Jack. "I should not wonder at all if this is Fairyland. So as the boat came here to please me, I shall ask it to stay where it is, in case I should want it again."

So he sprang ashore, and said to the boat, 27 "Stay just where you are, will you?" and he ran after the old women, calling to them,—

"Is there any law to prevent my coming into your country?"

"Wo!" cried the red-coated old woman, and the horse stopped, while the blue-coated woman repeated, "Any law? No, not that I know of; but if you are a stranger here you had better look out."

"Why?" asked Jack.

"You don't suppose, do you," she answered, "that our Queen will wind up strangers?"

While Jack was wondering what she meant, the other said,—

"I shouldn't wonder if he goes eight days. Gee!" and the horse went on.

"No, wo!" said the other.

"No, no. Gee! I tell you," cried the first.

Upon this, to Jack's intense astonishment, the old horse stopped, and said, speaking through his nose,—

"Now, then, which is it to be? I'm willing to 28 gee, and I'm agreeable to wo; but what's a fellow to do when you say them both together?"

"Why, he talks!" exclaimed Jack.

"It's because he's got a cold in his head," observed one of the washer-women; "he always talks when he's got a cold, and there's no pleasing him; whatever you say, he's not satisfied. Gee, Boney, do!"

"Gee it is, then," said the horse, and began to jog on.

"He spoke again!" said Jack, upon which the horse laughed, and Jack was quite alarmed.

"It appears that your horses don't talk?" observed the blue-coated woman.

"Never," answered Jack; "they can't."

"You mean they won't," observed the old horse; and though he spoke the words of mankind, it was not in a voice like theirs. Still Jack felt that his was just the natural tone for a horse, and that it did not arise only from the length of his nose. "You'll find out some day, perhaps," he continued, "whether horses can talk or not."

"Shall I?" said Jack, very earnestly.

"They'll TELL," proceeded the white horse. "I wouldn't be you when they tell how you've used them."

"Have you been ill used?" said Jack, in an anxious tone.

"Yes, yes, of course he has," one of the women broke in; "but he has come here to get all right again. This is a very wholesome country for horses; isn't it, Boney?"

"Yes," said the horse.

"Well, then, jog on, there's a dear," continued the old woman. "Why, you will be young again soon, you know,—young, and gamesome, and handsome; you'll be quite a colt, by and by, and then we shall set you free to join your companions in the happy meadows."

The old horse was so comforted by this kind speech, that he pricked up his ears and quickened his pace considerably.

"He was shamefully used," observed one washer-woman. 30 "Look at him, how lean he is! You can see all his ribs."

"Yes," said the other, as if apologizing for the poor old horse. "He gets low-spirited when he thinks of all he has gone through; but he is a vast deal better already than he was. He used to live in London; his master always carried a long whip to beat him with, and never spoke civilly to him."

"London!" exclaimed Jack; "why that is in my country. How did the horse get here?"

"That's no business of yours," answered one of the women. "But I can tell you he came because he was wanted, which is more than you are."

"You let him alone," said the horse, in a querulous tone. "I don't bear any malice."

"No; he has a good disposition, has Boney," observed the red old woman. "Pray, are you a boy?"

"Yes," said Jack.

"A real boy, that wants no winding up?" inquired the old woman.

"I don't know what you mean," answered Jack; "but I am a real boy, certainly."

"Ah!" she replied. "Well, I thought you were, by the way Boney spoke to you. How frightened you must be! I wonder what will be done to all your people for driving, and working, and beating so many beautiful creatures to death every year that comes? They'll have to pay for it some day, you may depend."

Jack was a little alarmed, and answered that he had never been unkind himself to horses, and he was glad that Boney bore no malice.

"They worked him, and often drove him about all night in the miserable streets, and never let him have so much as a canter in a green field," said one of the women; "but he'll be all right now, only he has to begin at the wrong end."

"What do you mean?" said Jack.

"Why, in this country," answered the old woman, "they begin by being terribly old and stiff, and they seem miserable and jaded at first, 32 but by degrees they get young again, as you heard me reminding him."

"Indeed," said Jack; "and do you like that?"

"It has nothing to do with me," she answered. "We are only here to take care of all the creatures that men have ill used. While they are sick and old, which they are when first they come to us,—after they are dead, you know,—we take care of them, and gradually bring them up to be young and happy again."

"This must be a very nice country to live in, then," said Jack.

"For horses it is," said the old lady, significantly.

"Well," said Jack, "it does seem very full of haystacks, certainly, and all the air smells of fresh grass."

At this moment they came to a beautiful meadow, and the old horse stopped, and, turning to the blue-coated woman, said, "Faxa, I think I could fancy a handful of clover." Upon this Faxa snatched Jack's cap off his head, and in a very 33 active manner jumped over a little ditch, and gathering some clover, presently brought it back full, handing it to the old horse with great civility.

"You shouldn't be in such a hurry," observed the old horse; "your weights will be running down some day, if you don't mind."

"It's all zeal," observed the red-coated woman.

Just then a little man, dressed like a groom, came running up, out of breath. "Oh, here you are, Dow!" he exclaimed to the red-coated woman. "Come along, will you? Lady Betty wants you; it's such a hot day, and nobody, she says, can fan her so well as you can."

The red-coated woman, without a word, went off with the groom, and Jack thought he would go with them, for this Lady Betty could surely tell him whether the country was called Fairyland, or whether he must get into his boat and go farther. He did not like either to hear the way in which Faxa and Dow talked about their works and their weights; so he asked Faxa to give him his cap, which she did, and he heard a curious sort of little 34 ticking noise as he came close to her, which startled him.

"Oh, this must be Fairyland, I am sure," thought Jack, "for in my country our pulses beat quite differently from that."

"Well," said Faxa, rather sharply, "do you find any fault with the way I go?"

"No," said Jack, a little ashamed of having listened. "I think you walk beautifully; your steps are so regular."

"She's machine-made," observed the old horse, in a melancholy voice, and with a deep sigh. "In the largest magnifying-glass you'll hardly find the least fault with her chain. She's not like the goods they turn out in Clerkenwell."

Jack was more and more startled, and so glad to get his cap and run after the groom and Dow to find Lady Betty, that he might be with ordinary human beings again; but when he got up to them, he found that Lady Betty was a beautiful brown mare! She was lying in a languid and rather affected attitude, with a load of fresh hay before 35 her, and two attendants, one of whom stood holding a parasol over her head, and the other was fanning her.

"I'm so glad you are come, my good Dow," said the brown mare. "Don't you think I am strong enough to-day to set off for the happy meadows?"

"Well," said Dow, "I'm afraid not yet; you must remember that it is of no use your leaving us till you have quite got over the effects of the fall."

Just then Lady Betty observed Jack, and said, "Take that boy away; he reminds me of a jockey."

The attentive groom instantly started forward, but Jack was too nimble for him; he ran and ran with all his might, and only wished he had never left the boat. But still he heard the groom behind him; and in fact the groom caught him at last, and held him so fast that struggling was of no use at all.

"You young rascal!" he exclaimed, as he recovered breath. "How you do run! It's enough to break your mainspring."

"What harm did I do?" asked Jack. "I was only looking at the mare."

"Harm!" exclaimed the groom; "harm indeed! Why, you reminded her of a jockey. It's enough to hold her back, poor thing!—and we trying so hard, too, to make her forget what a cruel end she came to in the old world."

"You need not hold me so tightly," said Jack, "I shall not run away again; but," he added, "if this is Fairyland, it is not half such a nice country as I expected."

"Fairyland!" exclaimed the groom, stepping back with surprise. "Why, what made you think of such a thing? This is only one of the border countries, where things are set right again that people have caused to go wrong in the world. The world, you know, is what men and women call their own home."

"I know," said Jack; "and that's where I came from." Then, as the groom seemed no longer to be angry, he went on: "And I wish you would tell me about Lady Betty."

"She was a beautiful fleet creature, of the racehorse breed," said the groom; "and she won silver cups for her master, and then they made her run a steeple-chase, which frightened her, but still she won it; and then they made her run another, and she cleared some terribly high hurdles, and many gates and ditches, till she came to an awful one, and at first she would not take it, but her rider spurred and beat her till she tried. It was beyond her powers, and she fell and broke both her forelegs. Then they shot her. After she had died that miserable death, we had her here, to make her all right again."

"Is this the only country where you set things right?" asked Jack.

"Certainly not," answered the groom; "they lie about in all directions. Why, you might wander for years, and never come to the end of this one."

"I am afraid I shall not find the one I am looking for," said Jack, "if your countries are so large."

"I don't think our world is much larger than yours," answered the groom. "But come along: I hear the bell, and we are a good way from the palace."

Jack, in fact, heard the violent ringing of a bell at some distance; and when the groom began to run, he ran beside him, for he thought he should like to see the palace. As they ran, people gathered from all sides,—fields, cottages, mills,—till at last there was a little crowd, among whom Jack saw Dow and Faxa, and they were all making for a large house, the wide door of which was standing open. Jack stood with the crowd, and peeped in. There was a woman sitting inside upon a rocking-chair,—a tall, large woman, with a gold-colored gown on,—and beside her stood a table, covered with things that looked like keys.

"What is that woman doing?" said he to Faxa, who was standing close to him.

"Winding us up, to be sure," answered Faxa. "You don't suppose, surely, that we can go forever?"

"Extraordinary!" said Jack. "Then are you wound up every evening, like watches?"
"Unless we have misbehaved ourselves," she answered; "and then she lets us run down."
"And what then?"
"What then?" repeated Faxa, "why, then we have to stop and stand against a wall, till she is pleased to forgive us, and let our friends carry us in to be set going again."

Jack looked in, and saw the people pass in and stand close by the woman. One after the other she took by the chin with her left hand, and with her right hand found a key that pleased her. It seemed to Jack that there was a tiny key-hole in the back of their heads, and that she put the key in and wound them up.

"You must take your turn with the others," said the groom.

"There's no key-hole in my head," said Jack; 40 "besides, I do not want any woman to wind me up."

"But you must do as others do," he persisted; "and if you have no key-hole, our Queen can easily have one made, I should think."

"Make one in my head!" exclaimed Jack. "She shall do no such thing."

"We shall see," said Faxa, quietly. And Jack was so frightened that he set off, and ran back towards the river with all his might. Many of the people called to him to stop, but they could not run after him, because they wanted winding up. However, they would certainly have caught him if he had not been very quick, for before he got to the river he heard behind him the footsteps of those who had been first attended to by the Queen, and he had only just time to spring into the boat when they reached the edge of the water.

No sooner was he on board than the boat swung round, and got out again into the middle of the stream; but he could not feel safe till not only was there a long reach of water between him and the 41 shore, but till he had gone so far down the river that the beautiful bay had passed out of sight, and the sun was going down. By this time he began to feel very tired and sleepy; so, having looked at his fairies, and found that they were all safe and fast asleep, he laid down in the bottom of the boat, and fell into a doze, and then into a dream.

CHAPTER IV. BEES AND OTHER FELLOW-CREATURES.

The dove laid some little sticks, Then began to coo; The gnat took his trumpet up To play the day through; The pie chattered soft and long— But that she always does; The bee did all he had to do, And only said, "Buzz."

When Jack at length opened his eyes, he found that it was night, for the full moon was shining; but it was not at all a dark night, for he could see distinctly some black birds, that looked like ravens. They were sitting in a row on the edge of the boat.

Now that he had fairies in his pockets, he could 43 understand bird-talk, and he heard one of these ravens saying, "There is no meat so tender; I wish I could pick their little eyes out."

"Yes," said another, "fairies are delicate eating indeed. We must speak Jack fair if we want to get at them." And she heaved up a deep sigh.

Jack lay still, and thought he had better pretend to be asleep; but they soon noticed that his eyes were open, and one of them presently walked up his leg and bowed, and asked if he was hungry.

Jack said, "No."

"No more am I," replied the raven; "not at all hungry." Then she hopped off his leg, and Jack sat up.

"And how are the sweet fairies that my young master is taking to their home?" asked another of the ravens. "I hope they are safe in my young master's pockets?"

Jack felt in his pockets. Yes, they were all safe; but he did not take any of them out, lest the ravens should snatch at them.

"Eh?" continued the raven, pretending to listen; 44 "did this dear young gentleman say that the fairies were asleep?"

"It doesn't amuse me to talk about fairies," said Jack; "but if you would explain some of the things in this country that I cannot make out, I should be very glad."

"What things?" asked the blackest of the ravens.

"Why," said Jack, "I see a full moon lying down there among the water-flags, and just going to set, and there is a half-moon overhead plunging among those great gray clouds, and just this moment I saw a thin crescent moon peeping out between the branches of that tree."

"Well," said all the ravens at once, "did the young master never see a crescent moon in the men and women's world?"

"Oh yes," said Jack.

"Did he never see a full moon?" asked the ravens.

"Yes, of course," said Jack; "but they are the same moon. I could never see all three of them at the same time."

The ravens were very much surprised at this, and one of them said,—

"If my young master did not see the moons it must have been because he didn't look. Perhaps my young master slept in a room, and had only one window; if so, he couldn't see all the sky at once."

"I tell you, Raven," said Jack, laughing, "that I KNOW there is never more than one moon in my country, and sometimes there is no moon at all!"

Upon this all the ravens hung down their heads, and looked very much ashamed; for there is nothing that birds hate so much as to be laughed at, and they believed that Jack was saying this to mock them, and that he knew what they had come for. So first one and then another hopped to the other end of the boat and flew away, till at last there was only one left, and she appeared to be out of spirits, and did not speak again till he spoke to her.

"Raven," said Jack, "there's something very 46 cold and slippery lying at the bottom of the boat. I touched it just now, and I don't like it at all."

"It's a water-snake," said the raven; and she stooped and picked up a long thing with her beak, which she threw out, and then looked over. "The water swarms with them, wicked, murderous creatures; they smell the young fairies, and they want to eat them."

Jack was so thrown off his guard that he snatched one fairy out, just to make sure that it was safe. It was the one with the mustache; and, alas! in one instant the raven flew at it, got it out of his hand, and pecked off its head before it had time to wake or Jack to rescue it. Then, as she slowly rose, she croaked, and said to Jack, "You'll catch it for this, my young master!" and she flew to the bough of a tree, where she finished eating the fairy, and threw his little empty coat into the river.

On this Jack began to cry bitterly, and to think what a foolish boy he had been. He was the more sorry because he did not even know that 47 poor little fellow's name. But he had heard the others calling by name to their companions, and very grand names they were too. One was Jovinian,—he was a very fierce-looking gentleman; the other two were Roxaletta and Mopsa.

Presently, however, Jack forgot to be unhappy, for two of the moons went down, and then the sun rose, and he was delighted to find that however many moons there might be, there was only one sun, even in the country of the wonderful river.

So on and on they went; but the river was very wide, and the waves were boisterous. On the right brink was a thick forest of trees, with such heavy foliage that a little way off they looked like a bank, green, and smooth, and steep; but as the light became clearer, Jack could see here and there the great stems, and see creatures like foxes, wild boars, and deer, come stealing down to drink in the river.

It was very hot here; not at all like the spring weather he had left behind. And as the low 48 sunbeams shone into Jack's face he said hastily, without thinking of what would occur, "I wish I might land among those lovely glades on the left bank."

No sooner said than the boat began to make for the left bank, and the nearer they got towards it the more beautiful it became; but also the more stormy were the reaches of water they had to traverse.

A lovely country indeed! It sloped gently down to the water's edge, and beautiful trees were scattered over it, soft, mossy grass grew everywhere, great old laburnum trees stretched their boughs down in patches over the water, and higher up camellias, almost as large as hawthorns, grew together and mingled their red and white flowers.

The country was not so open as a park,—it was more like a half-cleared woodland; but there was a wide space just where the boat was steering for, that had no trees, only a few flowering shrubs. Here groups of strange-looking people were bustling 49 about, and there were shrill fifes sounding, and drums.

Farther back he saw rows of booths or tents under the shade of the trees.

In another place some people dressed like gypsies had made fires of sticks just at the skirts of the woodland, and were boiling their pots. Some of these had very gaudy tilted carts, hung all over with goods, such as baskets, brushes, mats, little glasses, pottery, and beads.

It seemed to be a kind of fair, to which people had gathered from all parts; but there was not one house to be seen. All the goods were either hung upon trees or collected in strange-looking tents.

The people were not all of the same race; indeed, he thought the only human beings were the gypsies, for the folks who had tents were no taller than himself.

How hot it was that morning! and as the boat pushed itself into a little creek, and made its way among the beds of yellow and purple iris which 50 skirted the brink, what a crowd of dragon-flies and large butterflies rose from them!

"Stay where you are!" cried Jack to the boat; and at that instant such a splendid moth rose slowly, that he sprang on shore after it, and quite forgot the fair and the people in his desire to follow it.

The moth settled on a great red honey-flower, and he stole up to look at it. As large as a swallow, it floated on before him. Its wings were nearly black, and they had spots of gold on them.

When it rose again Jack ran after it, till he found himself close to the rows of tents where the brown people stood; and they began to cry out to him, "What'll you buy? what'll you buy, sir?" and they crowded about him, so that he soon lost sight of the moth, and forgot everything else in his surprise at the booths.

They were full of splendid things,—clocks and musical boxes, strange china ornaments, embroidered slippers, red caps, and many kinds of splendid silks and small carpets. In other booths 51 were swords and dirks, glittering with jewels; and the chatter of the people when they talked together was not in a language that Jack could understand.

Some of the booths were square, and evidently made of common canvas, for when you went into them, and the sun shone, you could distinctly see the threads.

But scattered a little farther on in groups were some round tents, which were far more curious. They were open on all sides, and consisted only of a thick canopy overhead, which was supported by one beautiful round pillar in the middle.

Outside the canopy was white or brownish; but when Jack stood under these tents, he saw that they were lined with splendid flutings of brown or pink silk: what looked like silk, at least, for it was impossible to be sure whether these were real tents or gigantic mushrooms.

They varied in size, also, as mushrooms do, and in shape: some were large enough for twenty people to stand under them, and had flat tops 52 with a brown lining; others had dome-shaped roofs; these were lined with pink, and would only shelter six or seven.

The people who sold in these tents were as strange as their neighbors; each had a little high cap on his head, in shape just like a beehive, and it was made of straw, and had a little hole in front. In fact, Jack very soon saw bees flying in and out, and it was evident that these people had their honey made on the premises. They were chiefly selling country produce. They had cheeses so large as to reach to their waists, and the women trundled them along as boys do their hoops. They sold a great many kinds of seed, too, in wooden bowls, and cakes and good things to eat, such as gilt gingerbread. Jack bought some of this, and found it very nice indeed. But when he took out his money to pay for it, the little man looked rather strangely at it, and turned it over with an air of disgust. Then Jack saw him hand it to his wife, who also seemed to dislike it; and presently Jack observed that they followed 53 him about, first on one side, then on the other. At last, the little woman slipped her hand into his pocket, and Jack, putting his hand in directly, found his sixpence had been returned.

"Why, you've given me back my money!" he said.

The little woman put her hands behind her. "I do not like it," she said; "it's dirty; at least, it's not new."

"No, it's not new," said Jack, a good deal surprised, "but it is a good sixpence."

"The bees don't like it," continued the little woman. "They like things to be neat and new, and that sixpence is bent."

"What shall I give you then?" said Jack.

The good little woman laughed and blushed. "This young gentleman has a beautiful whistle round his neck," she observed, politely, but did not ask for it.

Jack had a dog-whistle, so he took it off and gave it to her.

"Thank you for the bees," she said. "They 54 love to be called home when we've collected flowers for them."

So she made a pretty little courtesy, and went away to her customers.

There were some very strange creatures also, about the same height as Jack, who had no tents, and seemed there to buy, not to sell. Yet they looked poorer than the other folks, and they were also very cross and discontented; nothing pleased them. Their clothes were made of moss, and their mantles of feathers; and they talked in a queer whistling tone of voice, and carried their skinny little children on their backs and on their shoulders.

They were treated with great respect by the people in the tents; and when Jack asked his friend to whom he had given the whistle what they were, and where they got so much money as they had, she replied that they lived over the hills, and were afraid to come in their best clothes. They were rich and powerful at home, and they came shabbily dressed, and behaved humbly, lest their 55 enemies should envy them. It was very dangerous, she said, to fairies to be envied.

Jack wanted to listen to their strange whistling talk, but he could not for the noise and cheerful chattering of the brown folks, and more still for the screaming and talking of parrots.

Among the goods were hundreds of splendid gilt cages, which were hung by long gold chains from the trees. Each cage contained a parrot and his mate, and they all seemed to be very unhappy indeed.

The parrots could talk, and they kept screaming to the discontented women to buy things for them, and trying very hard to attract attention.

One old parrot made himself quite conspicuous by these efforts. He flung himself against the wires of his cage, he squalled, he screamed, he knocked the floor with his beak, till Jack and one of the customers came running up to see what was the matter.

"What do you make such a fuss for?" cried the discontented woman. "You've set your cage 56 swinging with knocking yourself about; and what good does that do? I cannot break the spell and open it for you."

"I know that," answered the parrot, sobbing; "but it hurts my feelings so that you should take no notice of me now that I have come down in the world."

"Yes," said the parrot's mate, "it hurts our feelings."

"I haven't forgotten you," answered the woman, more crossly than ever; "I was buying a measure of maize for you when you began to make such a noise."

Jack thought this was the queerest conversation he had ever heard in his life; and he was still more surprised when the bird answered,—

"I would much rather you would buy me a pocket-handkerchief. Here we are, shut up, without a chance of getting out, and with nobody to pity us; and we can't even have the comfort of crying, because we've got nothing to wipe our eyes with."

"But at least," replied the woman, "you CAN cry now if you please, and when you had your other face you could not."

"Buy me a handkerchief," sobbed the parrot.

"I can't afford both," whined the cross woman, "and I've paid now for the maize." So saying, she went back to the tent to fetch her present to the parrots; and as their cage was still swinging Jack put out his hand to steady it for them, and the instant he did so they became perfectly silent, and all the other parrots on that tree, who had been flinging themselves about in their cages, left off screaming, and became silent too.

The old parrot looked very cunning. His cage hung by such a long gold chain that it was just on a level with Jack's face, and so many odd things had happened that day that it did not seem more odd than usual to hear him say, in a tone of great astonishment,—

"It's a BOY, if ever there was one!"

"Yes," said Jack; "I'm a boy."

"You won't go yet, will you?" said the parrot.

"No, don't," said a great many other parrots. Jack agreed to stay a little while, upon which they all thanked him.

"I had no notion you were a boy till you touched my cage," said the old parrot.

Jack did not know how this could have told him, so he only answered, "Indeed!"

"I'm a fairy," observed the parrot, in a confidential tone. "We are imprisoned here by our enemies the gypsies."

"So we are," answered a chorus of other parrots.

"I'm sorry for that," replied Jack. "I'm friends with the fairies."

"Don't tell," said the parrot, drawing a film over his eyes, and pretending to be asleep. At that moment his friend in the moss petticoat and feather cloak came up with a little measure of maize, and poured it into the cage.

"Here, neighbor," she said; "I must say good-by now, for the gypsy is coming this way, and I want to buy some of her goods."

"Well, thank you," answered the parrot, sobbing 59 again; "but I could have wished it had been a pocket-handkerchief."

"I'll lend you my handkerchief," said Jack. "Here!" And he drew it out, and pushed it between the wires.

The parrot and his wife were in a great hurry to get Jack's handkerchief. They pulled it in very hastily; but instead of using it they rolled it up into a ball, and the parrot-wife tucked it under her wing.

"It makes me tremble all over," said she, "to think of such good luck."

"I say," observed the parrot to Jack, "I know all about it now. You've got some of my people in your pockets,—not of my own tribe, but fairies."

By this Jack was sure that the parrot really was a fairy himself, and he listened to what he had to say the more attentively.

CHAPTER V. THE PARROT IN HIS SHAWL.

That handkerchief Did an Egyptian to my mother give; She was a charmer, and could almost read The thoughts of people.—Othello.

"That gypsy woman who is coming with her cart," said the parrot, "is a fairy too, and very malicious. It was she and others of her tribe who caught us and put us into these cages, for they are more powerful than we. Mind you do not let her allure you into the woods, nor wheedle you or frighten you into giving her any of those fairies."

"No," said Jack; "I will not."

"She sold us to the brown people," continued the parrot. "Mind you do not buy anything of 61 her, for your money in her palm would act as a charm against you."

"She has a baby," observed the parrot-wife, scornfully.

"Yes, a baby," repeated the old parrot; "and I hope by means of that baby to get her driven away, and perhaps get free myself. I shall try to put her in a passion. Here she comes."

There she was indeed, almost close at hand. She had a little cart; her goods were hung all about it, and a small horse drew it slowly on, and stopped when she got a customer.

Several gypsy children were with her, and as the people came running together over the grass to see her goods, she sang a curious kind of song, which made them wish to buy them.

Jack turned from the parrot's cage as she came up. He had heard her singing a little way off, and now, before she began again, he felt that already her searching eyes had found him out, and taken notice that he was different from the other people.

When she began to sing her selling song, he felt a most curious sensation. He felt as if there were some cobwebs before his face, and he put up his hand as if to clear them away. There were no real cobwebs, of course; and yet he again felt as if they floated from the gypsy woman to him, like gossamer threads, and attracted him towards her. So he gazed at her, and she at him, till Jack began to forget how the parrot had warned him.

He saw her baby too, wondered whether it was heavy for her to carry, and wished he could help her. I mean, he saw that she had a baby on her arm. It was wrapped in a shawl, and had a handkerchief over its face. She seemed very fond of it, for she kept hushing it; and Jack softly moved nearer and nearer to the cart, till the gypsy woman smiled, and suddenly began to sing,—

My good man—he's an old, old man And my good man got a fall, To buy me a bargain so fast he ran When he heard the gypsies call: "Buy, buy brushes, Baskets wrought o' rushes. Buy them, buy them, take them, try them, Buy, dames all."

63 My old man, he has money and land, And a young, young wife am I. Let him put the penny in my white hand When he hears the gypsies cry: "Buy, buy laces, Veils to screen your faces. Buy them, buy them, take and try them. Buy, maids, buy."

When the gypsy had finished her song, Jack felt as if he was covered all over with cobwebs; but he could not move away, and he did not mind them now. All his wish was to please her, and get close to her; so when she said, in a soft, wheedling voice, "What will you please to buy, my pretty gentleman?" he was just going to answer that he would buy anything she recommended, when, to his astonishment and displeasure, for he thought it very rude, the parrot suddenly burst into a violent fit of coughing, which made all the customers stare. "That's to clear my throat," he said, in a most impertinent tone of voice; and then he began to beat time with his foot, and sing, or rather scream out, an extremely saucy imitation of the gypsy's song, and 64 all his parrot friends in the other cages joined in the chorus.

My fair lady's a dear, dear lady— I walked by her side to woo. In a garden alley, so sweet and shady, She answered, "I love not you, John, John Brady," Quoth my dear lady, "Pray now, pray now, go your way now, Do, John, do!"

At first the gypsy did not seem to know where that mocking song came from, but when she discovered that it was her prisoner, the old parrot, who was thus daring to imitate her, she stood silent and glared at him, and her face was almost white with rage.

When he came to the end of the verse he pretended to burst into a violent fit of sobbing and crying, and screeched out to his wife, "Mate! mate! hand up my handkerchief. Oh! oh! it's so affecting, this song is."

Upon this the other parrot pulled Jack's handkerchief from under her wing, hobbled up, and 65 began, with a great show of zeal, to wipe his horny beak with it. But this was too much for the gypsy; she took a large brush from her cart, and flung it at the cage with all her might.

This set it violently swinging backwards and forwards, but did not stop the parrot, who screeched out, "How delightful it is to be swung!" And then he began to sing another verse in the most impudent tone possible, and with a voice that seemed to ring through Jack's head, and almost pierce it:—

Yet my fair lady's my own, own lady, For I passed another day; While making her moan, she sat all alone, And thus and thus did she say: "John, John Brady," Quoth my dear lady, "Do now, do now, once more woo now, Pray, John, pray!"

"It's beautiful!" screeched the parrot-wife, "and so ap-pro-pri-ate." Jack was delighted when she managed slowly to say this long word with her black tongue, and he burst out laughing. 66 In the mean time a good many of the brown people came running together, attracted by the noise of the parrots and the rage of the gypsy, who flung at his cage, one after the other, all the largest things she had in her cart. But nothing did the parrot any harm; the more violently his cage swung, the louder he sang, till at last the wicked gypsy seized her poor little young baby, who was lying in her arms, rushed frantically at the cage as it flew swiftly through the air towards her, and struck at it with the little creature's head. "Oh, you cruel, cruel woman!" cried Jack, and all the small mothers who were standing near with their skinny children on their shoulders, screamed out with terror and indignation; but only for one instant, for the handkerchief flew off that had covered its face, and was caught in the wires of the cage, and all the people saw that it was not a real baby at all, but a bundle of clothes, and its head was a turnip.

Yes, a turnip! You could see that as plainly as possible, for though the green leaves had been 67 cut off, their stalks were visible through the lace cap that had been tied on it.

Upon this all the crowd pressed closer, throwing her baskets, and brushes, and laces, and beads at the gypsy, and calling out, "We will have none of your goods, you false woman! Give us back our money, or we will drive you out of the fair. You've stuck a stick into a turnip, and dressed it up in baby clothes. You're a cheat! a cheat!"

"My sweet gentlemen, my kind ladies," began the gypsy; but baskets and brushes flew at her so fast that she was obliged to sit down on the grass and hold up the sham baby to screen her face.

While this was going on, Jack felt that the cobwebs which had seemed to float about his face were all gone; he did not care at all any more about the gypsy, and began to watch the parrots with great attention.

He observed that when the handkerchief stuck between the cage wires, the parrots caught it, and drew it inside; and then Jack saw the cunning 68 old bird himself lay it on the floor, fold it crosswise like a shawl, and put it on his wife.

Then she jumped upon the perch, and held it with one foot, looking precisely like an old lady with a parrot's head. Then he folded Jack's handkerchief in the same way, put it on, and got upon the perch beside his wife, screaming out, in his most piercing tone,—

"I like shawls; they're so becoming."

Now the gypsy did not care at all what those inferior people thought of her, and she was calmly counting out their money, to return it; but she was very desirous to make Jack forget her behavior, and had begun to smile again, and tell him she had only been joking, when the parrot spoke, and, looking up, she saw the two birds sitting side by side, and the parrot-wife was screaming in her mate's ear, though neither of them was at all deaf,—

"If Jack lets her allure him into the woods, he'll never come out again. She'll hang him up 69 in a cage, as she did us. I say, how does my shawl fit?"

So saying, the parrot-wife whisked herself round on the perch, and lo! in the corner of the handkerchief were seen some curious letters, marked in red. When the crowd saw these, they drew a little farther off, and glanced at one another with alarm.

"You look charming, my dear; it fits well!" screamed the old parrot in answer. "A word in your ear; 'Share and share alike' is a fine motto."

"What do you mean by all this?" said the gypsy, rising, and going with slow steps to the cage, and speaking cautiously.

"Jack," said the parrot, "do they ever eat handkerchiefs in your part of the country?"

"No, never," answered Jack.

"Hold your tongue and be reasonable," said the gypsy, trembling. "What do you want? I'll do it, whatever it is."

"But do they never pick out the marks?" continued 70 the parrot. "O Jack! are you sure they never pick out the marks?"

"The marks?" said Jack, considering. "Yes, perhaps they do."

"Stop!" cried the gypsy, as the old parrot made a peck at the strange letters. "Oh! you're hurting me. What do you want? I say again, tell me what you want, and you shall have it."

"We want to get out," replied the parrot; "you must undo the spell."

"Then give me my handkerchief," answered the gypsy, "to bandage my eyes. I dare not say the words with my eyes open. You had no business to steal it. It was woven by human hands, so that nobody can see through it; and if you don't give it to me, you'll never get out,—no, never!"

"Then," said the old parrot, tossing his shawl off, "you may have Jack's handkerchief; it will bandage your eyes just as well. It was woven over the water, as yours was."

"It won't do!" cried the gypsy, in terror; "give me my own."

"I tell you," answered the parrot, "that you shall have Jack's handkerchief; you can do no harm with that."

By this time the parrots all around had become perfectly silent, and none of the people ventured to say a word, for they feared the malice of the gypsy. She was trembling dreadfully, and her dark eyes, which had been so bright and piercing, had become dull and almost dim; but when she found there was no help for it, she said,—

"Well, pass out Jack's handkerchief. I will set you free if you will bring out mine with you."

"Share and share alike," answered the parrot; "you must let all my friends out too."

"Then I won't let you out," answered the gypsy. "You shall come out first, and give me my handkerchief, or not one of their cages will I undo. So take your choice."

"My friends, then," answered the brave old 72 parrot; and he poked Jack's handkerchief out to her through the wires.

The wondering crowd stood by to look, and the gypsy bandaged her eyes tightly with the handkerchief; and then, stooping low, she began to murmur something and clap her hands—softly at first, but by degrees more and more violently. The noise was meant to drown the words she muttered; but as she went on clapping, the bottom of cage after cage fell clattering down. Out flew the parrots by hundreds, screaming and congratulating one another; and there was such a deafening din that not only the sound of her spell, but the clapping of her hands, was quite lost in it.

But all this time Jack was very busy; for the moment the gypsy had tied up her eyes, the old parrot snatched the real handkerchief off his wife's shoulders, and tied it round her neck. Then she pushed out her head through the wires, and the old parrot called to Jack, and said, "Pull!"

Jack took the ends of the handkerchief, pulled 73 terribly hard, and stopped. "Go on! go on!" screamed the old parrot.

"I shall pull her head off," cried Jack.

"No matter," cried the parrot; "no matter,—only pull."

Well, Jack did pull, and he actually did pull her head off! nearly tumbling backward himself as he did it; but he saw what the whole thing meant then, for there was another head inside,—a fairy's head.

Jack flung down the old parrot's head and great beak, for he saw that what he had to do was to clear the fairy of its parrot covering. The poor little creature seemed nearly dead, it was so terribly squeezed in the wires. It had a green gown or robe on, with an ermine collar; and Jack got hold of this dress, stripped the fairy out of the parrot feathers, and dragged her through,—velvet robe, and crimson girdle, and little yellow shoes. She was very much exhausted, but a kind brown woman took her instantly, and laid her in her 74 bosom. She was a splendid little creature, about half a foot long.

"There's a brave boy!" cried the parrot. Jack glanced round, and saw that not all the parrots were free yet, the gypsy was still muttering her spell.

He returned the handkerchief to the parrot, who put it round his own neck, and again Jack pulled. But oh! what a tough old parrot that was, and how Jack tugged before his cunning head would come off! It did, however, at last; and just as a fine fairy was pulled through, leaving his parrot skin and the handkerchief behind him, the gypsy untied her eyes, and saw what Jack had done.

"Give me my handkerchief!" she screamed, in despair.

"It's in the cage, gypsy," answered Jack; "you can get it yourself. Say your words again."

But the gypsy's spell would only open places where she had confined fairies, and no fairies were in the cage now.

"No, no, no!" she screamed; "too late! Hide me! O good people, hide me!"

But it was indeed too late. The parrots had been wheeling in the air, hundreds and hundreds of them, high above her head; and as she ceased speaking, she fell shuddering on the ground, drew her cloak over her face, and down they came, swooping in one immense flock, and settled so thickly all over her that she was completely covered; from her shoes to her head not an atom of her was to be seen.

All the people stood gravely looking on. So did Jack, but he could not see much for the fluttering of the parrots, nor hear anything for their screaming voices; but at last he made one of the cross people hear when he shouted to her, "What are they going to do to the poor gypsy?"

"Make her take her other form," she replied; "and then she cannot hurt us while she stays in our country. She is a fairy, as we have just found out, and all fairies have two forms."

"Oh!" said Jack; but he had no time for more questions.

The screaming and fighting, and tossing about of little bits of cloth and cotton, ceased; a black lump heaved itself up from the ground among the parrots; and as they flew aside, an ugly great condor, with a bare neck, spread out its wings, and, skimming the ground, sailed slowly away.

"They have pecked her so that she can hardly rise," exclaimed the parrot fairy. "Set me on your shoulder, Jack, and let me see the end of it."

Jack set him there; and his little wife, who had recovered herself, sprang from her friend the brown woman, and sat on the other shoulder. He then ran on,—the tribe of brown people and mushroom people, and the feather-coated folks running too,—after the great black bird, who skimmed slowly on before them till she got to the gypsy carts, when out rushed the gypsies, armed with poles, milking-stools, spades, and everything 77 they could get hold of to beat back the people and the parrots from hunting their relation, who had folded her tired wings, and was skulking under a cart, with ruffled feathers and a scowling eye.

Jack was so frightened at the violent way in which the gypsies and the other tribes were knocking each other about, that he ran off, thinking he had seen enough of such a dangerous country.

As he passed the place where that evil-minded gypsy had been changed, he found the ground strewed with little bits of her clothes. Many parrots were picking them up, and poking them into the cage where the handkerchief was; and presently another parrot came with a lighted brand, which she had pulled from one of the gypsies' fires.

"That's right," said the fairy on Jack's shoulder, when he saw his friend push the brand between the wires of what had been his cage, and set the gypsy's handkerchief on fire, and all the bits of her clothes with it. "She won't find much of herself here," he observed, as Jack went on. "It will not be very easy to put herself together again."

So Jack moved away. He was tired of the noise and confusion; and the sun was just setting as he reached the little creek where his boat lay.

Then the parrot fairy and his wife sprang down, and kissed their hands to him as he stepped on board, and pushed the boat off. He saw, when he looked back, that a great fight was still going on; so he was glad to get away, and he wished his two friends good-by, and set off, the old parrot fairly calling after him, "My relations have put some of our favorite food on board for you." Then they again thanked him for his good help, and sprang into a tree, and the boat began to go down the wonderful river.

"This has been a most extraordinary day," thought Jack; "the strangest day I have had yet." And after he had eaten a good supper of what the parrots had brought, he felt so tired and sleepy that he laid down in the boat, and presently fell fast asleep. His fairies were sound asleep too in his pockets, and nothing happened of the least consequence; so he slept comfortably till morning.

CHAPTER VI. THE TOWN WITH NOBODY IN IT.

"Master," quoth the auld hound, "Where will ye go?" "Over moss, over muir. To court my new jo." "Master, though the night be merk, I'se follow through the snow."

"Court her, master, court her, So shall ye do weel; But and ben she'll guide the house, I'se get milk and meal. Ye'se get lilting while she sits With her rock and reel."

"For, oh! she has a sweet tongue, And een that look down, A gold girdle for her waist, And a purple gown. She has a good word forbye Fra a' folk in the town."

Soon after sunrise they came to a great city, and it was perfectly still. There were grand towers and terraces, wharves, too, and a large 81 market, but there was nobody anywhere to be seen. Jack thought that might be because it was so early in the morning; and when the boat ran itself up against a wooden wharf and stopped, he jumped ashore, for he thought this must be the end of his journey. A delightful town it was, if only there had been any people in it! The market-place was full of stalls, on which were spread toys, baskets, fruit, butter, vegetables, and all the other things that are usually sold in a market.

Jack walked about in it. Then he looked in at the open doors of the houses, and at last, finding that they were all empty, he walked into one, looked at the rooms, examined the picture-books, rang the bells, and set the musical-boxes going. Then, after he had shouted a good deal, and tried in vain to make some one hear, he went back to the edge of the river where his boat was lying, and the water was so delightfully clear and calm, that he thought he would bathe. So he took off his clothes, and folding them very carefully, 82 so as not to hurt the fairies, laid them down beside a hay-cock, and went in, and ran about and paddled for a long time,—much longer than there was any occasion for; but then he had nothing to do.

When at last he had finished, he ran to the hay-cock and began to dress himself; but he could not find his stockings, and after looking about for some time he was obliged to put on his clothes without them, and he was going to put his boots on his bare feet, when, walking to the other side of the hay-cock, he saw a little old woman about as large as himself. She had a pair of spectacles on, and she was knitting.

She looked so sweet-tempered that Jack asked her if she knew anything about his stockings.

"It will be time enough to ask for them when you have had your breakfast," said she. "Sit down. Welcome to our town. How do you like it?"

JACK'S NEW FRIEND.

"She had a pair of spectacles on, and she was knitting."—.

"I should like it very much indeed," said Jack, "if there was anybody in it."

"I'm glad of that," said the woman. "You've seen a good deal of it; but it pleases me to find that you are a very honest boy. You did not take anything at all. I am honest too."

"Yes," said Jack, "of course you are."

"And as I am pleased with you for being honest," continued the little woman, "I shall give you some breakfast out of my basket." So she took out a saucer full of honey, a roll of bread, and a cup of milk.

"Thank you," said Jack, "but I am not a beggar-boy; I have got a half-crown, a shilling, a sixpence, and two pence; so I can buy this breakfast of you, if you like. You look very poor."

"Do I?" said the little woman, softly; and she went on knitting, and Jack began to eat the breakfast.

"I wonder what has become of my stockings," said Jack.

"You will never see them any more," said the old woman. "I threw them into the river, and they floated away."

"Why did you?" asked Jack.

The little woman took no notice; but presently she had finished a beautiful pair of stockings, and she handed them to Jack, and said,—

"Is that like the pair you lost?"

"Oh no," said Jack; "these are much more beautiful stockings than mine."

"Do you like them as well?" asked the fairy woman.

"I like them much better," said Jack, putting them on. "How clever you are!"

"Would you like to wear these," said the woman, "instead of yours?"

She gave Jack such a strange look when she said this, that he was afraid to take them, and answered,—

"I shouldn't like to wear them if you think I had better not."

"Well," she answered, "I am very honest, as I told you; and therefore I am obliged to say that if I were you I would not wear those stockings on any account."

"Why not?" said Jack; for she looked so sweet-tempered that he could not help trusting her.

"Why not?" repeated the fairy; "why, because when you have those stockings on, your feet belong to me."

"Oh!" said Jack. "Well, if you think that matters, I'll take them off again. Do you think it matters?"

"Yes," said the fairy woman; "it matters, because I am a slave, and my master can make me do whatever he pleases, for I am completely in his power. So, if he found out that I had knitted these stockings for you, he would make me order you to walk into his mill,—the mill which grinds the corn for the town; and there you would have to grind and grind till I got free again."

When Jack heard this, he pulled off the beautiful stockings, and laid them on the old woman's lap. Upon this she burst out crying, as if her heart would break.

"If my fairies that I have in my pocket would only wake," said Jack, "I would fight your master; for if he is no bigger than you are, perhaps I could beat him, and get you away."

"No, Jack," said the little woman; "that would be of no use. The only thing you could do would be to buy me; for my cruel master has said that if ever I am late again he shall sell me in the slave market to the brown people, who work underground. And, though I am dreadfully afraid of my master, I mean to be late to-day, in hopes (as you are kind, and as you have some money) that you will come to the slave-market and buy me. Can you buy me, Jack, to be your slave?"

"I don't want a slave," said Jack; "and, besides, I have hardly any money to buy you with."

"But it is real money," said the fairy woman, "not like what my master has. His money has to be made every week, for if there comes a hot day it cracks, so it never has time to look old, as your half-crown does; and that is how we know the real money, for we cannot imitate anything that is old. Oh, now, now it is twelve o'clock! now I am late again! and though I said I would do it, I am so frightened!"

So saying, the little woman ran off towards the town, wringing her hands, and Jack ran beside her.

"How am I to find your master?" he said.

"O Jack, buy me! buy me!" cried the fairy woman. "You will find me in the slave-market. Bid high for me. Go back and put your boots on, and bid high."

Now Jack had nothing on his feet, so he left the poor little woman to run into the town by herself, and went back to put his boots on. They were very uncomfortable, as he had no stockings; but he did not much mind that, and he counted his money. There was the half-crown that his grandmamma had given him on his birthday, 88 there was a shilling, a sixpence, and two pence, besides a silver fourpenny-piece which he had forgotten. He then marched into the town; and now it was quite full of people,—all of them little men and women about his own height. They thought he was somebody of consequence, and they called out to him to buy their goods. And he bought some stockings, and said, "What I want to buy now is a slave."

So they showed him the way to the slave-market, and there whole rows of odd-looking little people were sitting, while in front of them stood the slaves.

Now Jack had observed as he came along how very disrespectful the dogs of that town were to the people. They had a habit of going up to them and smelling at their legs, and even gnawing their feet as they sat before the little tables selling their wares; and what made this more surprising was that the people did not always seem to find out when they were being gnawed. But the moment the dogs saw Jack they came and fawned 89 on him, and two old hounds followed him all the way to the slave-market; and when he took a seat one of them laid down at his feet, and said, "Master, set your handsome feet on my back, that they may be out of the dust."

"Don't be afraid of him," said the other hound; "he won't gnaw your feet. He knows well enough that they are real ones."

"Are the other people's feet not real?" asked Jack.

"Of course not," said the hound. "They had a feud long ago with the fairies, and they all went one night into a great corn-field which belonged to these enemies of theirs, intending to steal the corn. So they made themselves invisible, as they are always obliged to do till twelve o'clock at noon; but before morning dawn, the wheat being quite ripe, down came the fairies with their sickles, surrounded the field, and cut the corn. So all their legs of course got cut off with it, for when they are invisible they cannot 90 stir. Ever since that they have been obliged to make their legs of wood."

While the hound was telling this story Jack looked about, but he did not see one slave who was in the least like his poor little friend, and he was beginning to be afraid that he should not find her, when he heard two people talking together.

"Good-day!" said one. "So you have sold that good-for-nothing slave of yours?"

"Yes," answered a very cross-looking old man. "She was late again this morning, and came to me crying and praying to be forgiven; but I was determined to make an example of her, so I sold her at once to Clink-of-the-Hole, and he has just driven her away to work in his mine."

Jack, on hearing this, whispered to the hound at his feet, "If you will guide me to Clink's hole, you shall be my dog."

"Master, I will do my best," answered the hound; and he stole softly out of the market, Jack following him.

CHAPTER VII. HALF-A-CROWN.

So useful it is to have money, heigh ho! So useful it is to have money!
A. H. Clough.

The old hound went straight through the town, smelling Clink's footsteps, till he came into a large field of barley; and there, sitting against a sheaf, for it was harvest time, they found Clink-of-the-Hole. He was a very ugly little brown man, and he was smoking a pipe in the shade; while crouched near him was the poor little woman, with her hands spread before her face.

"Good-day, sir," said Clink to Jack. "You are a stranger here, no doubt?"

"Yes," said Jack; "I only arrived this morning."

"Have you seen the town?" asked Clink, civilly; "there is a very fine market."

"Yes, I have seen the market," answered Jack. "I went into it to buy a slave, but I did not see one that I liked."

"Ah!" said Clink; "and yet they had some very fine articles." Here he pointed to the poor little woman, and said, "Now that's a useful body enough, and I had her very cheap."

"What did you give for her?" said Jack, sitting down.

"Three pitchers," said Clink, "and fifteen cups and saucers, and two shillings in the money of the town."

"Is their money like this?" said Jack, taking out his shilling.

When Clink saw the shilling he changed color, and said, very earnestly, "Where did you get that, dear sir?"

"Oh, it was given me," said Jack, carelessly.

Clink looked hard at the shilling, and so did the fairy woman, and Jack let them look some time, for he amused himself with throwing it up several times and catching it. At last he put it back in his pocket, and then Clink heaved a deep sigh. Then Jack took out a penny, and began to toss that up, upon which, to his great surprise, the little brown man fell on his knees, and said, "Oh, a shilling and a penny,—a shilling and a penny of mortal coin! What would I not give for a shilling and a penny!"

"I don't believe you have got anything to give," said Jack, cunningly; "I see nothing but that ring on your finger, and the old woman."

"But I have a great many things at home, sir," said the brown man, wiping his eyes; "and besides, that ring would be cheap at a shilling,—even a shilling of mortal coin."

"Would the slave be cheap at a penny?" said Jack.

"Would you give a penny for her, dear sir?" inquired Clink, trembling with eagerness.

"She is honest," answered Jack; "ask her whether I had better buy her with this penny."

"It does not matter what she says," replied the brown man; "I would sell twenty such as she is for a penny,—a real one."

"Ask her," repeated Jack; and the poor little woman wept bitterly, but she said, "No."

"Why not?" asked Jack; but she only hung down her head and cried.

"I'll make you suffer for this," said the brown man. But when Jack took out the shilling, and said, "Shall I buy you with this, slave?" his eyes actually shot out sparks, he was so eager.

"Speak!" he said to the fairy woman; "and if you don't say 'Yes,' I'll strike you."

"He cannot buy me with that," answered the fairy woman, "unless it is the most valuable coin he has got."

The brown man, on hearing this, rose up in a rage, and was just going to strike her a terrible blow, when Jack cried out, "Stop!" and took out his half-crown.

"Can I buy you with this?" said he; and the fairy woman answered, "Yes."

Upon this Clink drew a long breath, and his eyes grew bigger and bigger as he gazed at the half-crown.

"Shall she be my slave forever, and not yours," said Jack, "if I give you this?"

"She shall," said the brown man. And he made such a low bow, as he took the money, that his head actually knocked the ground. Then he jumped up; and, as if he was afraid Jack should repent of his bargain, he ran off towards the hole in the hill with all his might, shouting for joy as he went.

"Slave," said Jack, "that is a very ragged old apron that you have got, and your gown is quite worn out. Don't you think we had better spend my shilling in buying you some new clothes? You look so very shabby."

"Do I?" said the fairy woman, gently. "Well, master, you will do as you please."

"But you know better than I do," said Jack, "though you are my slave."

"You had better give me the shilling, then," answered the little old woman; "and then I advise you to go back to the boat, and wait there till I come."

"What!" said Jack; "can you go all the way back into the town again? I think you must be tired, for you know you are so very old."

The fairy woman laughed when Jack said this, and she had such a sweet laugh that he loved to hear it; but she took the shilling, and trudged off to the town, and he went back to the boat, his hound running after him.

He was a long time going, for he ran a good many times after butterflies, and then he climbed up several trees; and altogether he amused himself for such a long while that when he reached the boat his fairy woman was there before him. So he stepped on board, the hound followed, and the boat immediately began to swim on.

"Why, you have not bought any new clothes!" said Jack to his slave.

"No, master," answered the fairy woman; "but I have bought what I wanted." And she took out of her pocket a little tiny piece of purple ribbon, with a gold-colored satin edge, and a very small tortoise-shell comb.

When Jack saw these he was vexed, and said, "What do you mean by being so silly? I can't scold you properly, because I don't know what name to call you by, and I don't like to say 'Slave,' because that sounds so rude. Why, this bit of ribbon is such a little bit that it's of no use at all. It's not large enough even to make one mitten of."

"Isn't it?" said the slave. "Just take hold of it, master, and let us see if it will stretch."

So Jack did. And she pulled, and he pulled, and very soon the silk had stretched till it was nearly as large as a handkerchief; and then she shook it, and they pulled again. "This is very good fun," said Jack; "why now it is as large as an apron."

So she shook it again, and gave it a twitch here and a pat there; and then they pulled again, and the silk suddenly stretched so wide that Jack was very nearly falling overboard. So Jack's slave pulled off her ragged gown and apron, and put it on. It was a most beautiful robe of purple silk; it had a gold border, and it just fitted her.

JACK'S SLAVE.

"These are fairies," said Jack's slave; "but what are you?"—.

"That will do," she said. And then she took out the little tortoise-shell comb, pulled off her cap, and threw it into the river. She had a little knot of soft, gray hair, and she let it down, and began to comb. And as she combed the hair got much longer and thicker, till it fell in waves all about her throat. Then she combed again, and it all turned gold-color, and came tumbling down to her waist; and then she stood up in the boat, and combed once more, and shook out the hair, and there was such a quantity that it reached down to her feet, and she was so covered with it that you could not see one bit of her, excepting her eyes, which peeped out, and looked bright and full of tears.

Then she began to gather up her lovely locks; and when she had dried her eyes with them, she said, "Master, do you know what you have done? look at me now!" So she threw back the hair from her face, and it was a beautiful young face; and she looked so happy that Jack was glad he had bought her with his half-crown,—so glad that he could not help crying, and the fair slave cried too; and then instantly the little fairies woke, and sprang out of Jack's pockets. As they did so, Jovinian cried out, "Madam, I am your most humble servant"; and Roxaletta said, "I hope your Grace is well"; but the third got on Jack's knee, and took hold of the buttons of his waistcoat, and when the lovely slave looked at her, she hid her face and blushed with pretty childish shyness.

"These are fairies," said Jack's slave; "but what are you?"

"Jack kissed me," said the little thing; "and I want to sit on his knee."

"Yes," said Jack; "I took them out, and laid them in a row, to see that they were safe, and this one I kissed, because she looked such a little dear."

"Was she not like the others, then?" asked the slave.

"Yes," said Jack; "but I liked her the best; she was my favorite."

Now, the instant these three fairies sprang out of Jack's pockets, they got very much larger; in fact, they became fully grown,—that is to say, they measured exactly one foot one inch in height, which, as most people know, is exactly the proper height for fairies of that tribe. The two who had sprung out first were very beautifully dressed. One had a green velvet coat, and a sword, the hilt of which was incrusted with diamonds. The second had a white spangled robe, and the loveliest rubies and emeralds round her neck and in her hair; but the third, the one who sat on Jack's knee, had a white frock and a blue sash on. She had soft, fat arms, and a face just like that of a sweet little child.

When Jack's slave saw this, she took the little creature on her knee, and said to her, "How comes it that you are not like your companions?"

And she answered, in a pretty lisping voice, "It's because Jack kissed me."

"Even so it must be," answered the slave; "the love of a mortal works changes indeed. It is not often that we win anything so precious. Here, master, let her sit on your knee sometimes, and take care of her, for she cannot now take the same care of herself that others of her race are capable of."

So Jack let little Mopsa sit on his knee; and when he was tired of admiring his slave, and wondering at the respect with which the other two fairies treated her, and at their cleverness in getting water-lilies for her, and fanning her with feathers, he curled himself up in the bottom of 102 the boat with his own little favorite, and taught her how to play at cat's-cradle.

When they had been playing some time, and Mopsa was getting quite clever at the game, the lovely slave said, "Master, it is a long time since you spoke to me."

"And yet," said Jack, "there is something that I particularly want to ask you about."

"Ask it then," she replied.

"I don't like to have a slave," answered Jack; "and as you are so clever, don't you think you can find out how to be free again?"

"I am very glad you asked me about that," said the fairy woman. "Yes, master, I wish very much to be free; and as you were so kind as to give the most valuable piece of real money you possessed in order to buy me, I can be free if you can think of anything that you really like better than that half-crown, and if I can give it you."

"Oh, there are many things," said Jack. "I 103 like going up this river to Fairyland much better."

"But you are going there, master," said the fairy woman; "you were on the way before I met with you."

"I like this little child better," said Jack; "I love this little Mopsa. I should like her to belong to me."

"She is yours," answered the fairy woman; "she belongs to you already. Think of something else."

Jack thought again, and was so long about it that at last the beautiful slave said to him, "Master, do you see those purple mountains?"

Jack turned round in the boat, and saw a splendid range of purple mountains, going up and up. They were very great and steep, each had a crown of snow, and the sky was very red behind them, for the sun was going down.

"At the other side of those mountains is Fairyland," said the slave; "but if you cannot think of something that you should like better to 104 have than your half-crown, I can never enter in. The river flows straight up to yonder steep precipice, and there is a chasm in it which pierces it, and through which the river runs down beneath, among the very roots of the mountains, till it comes out at the other side. Thousands and thousands of the small people will come when they see the boat, each with a silken thread in his hand; but if there is a slave in it, not all their strength and skill can tow it through. Look at those rafts on the river; on them are the small people coming up."

Jack looked, and saw that the river was spotted with rafts, on which were crowded brown fairy sailors, each one with three green stripes on his sleeve, which looked like good conduct marks. All these sailors were chattering very fast, and the rafts were coming down to meet the boat.

"All these sailors to tow my slave!" said Jack. "I wonder, I do wonder, what you are?" But the fairy woman only smiled, and Jack went on: 105 "I have thought of something that I should like much better than my half-crown. I should like to have a little tiny bit of that purple gown of yours with the gold border."

Then the fairy woman said, "I thank you, master. Now I can be free." So she told Jack to lend her his knife, and with it she cut off a very small piece of the skirt of her robe, and gave it to him. "Now mind," she said, "I advise you never to stretch this unless you want to make some particular thing of it, for then it will only stretch to the right size; but if you merely begin to pull it for your own amusement, it will go on stretching and stretching, and I don't know where it will stop."

CHAPTER VIII. A STORY.

    In the night she told a story, In the night and all night through, While the moon was in her glory, And the branches dropped with dew.

    'Twas my life she told, and round it Rose the years as from a deep; In the world's great heart she found it, Cradled like a child asleep.

    In the night I saw her weaving By the misty moonbeam cold, All the weft her shuttle cleaving With a sacred thread of gold.

    Ah! she wept me tears of sorrow, Lulling tears so mystic sweet; Then she wove my last tomorrow, And her web lay at my feet.

    Of my life she made the story: I must weep—so soon 'twas told! But your name did lend it glory, And your love its thread of gold!

By this time, as the sun had gone down, and none of the moons had risen, it would have been dark but that each of the rafts was rigged 107 with a small mast that had a lantern hung to it.

By the light of these lanterns Jack saw crowds of little brown faces; and presently many rafts had come up to the boat, which was now swimming very slowly. Every sailor in every raft fastened to the boat's side a silken thread; then the rafts were rowed to shore, and the sailors jumped out, and began to tow the boat along.

A STORY.—.

These crimson threads looked no stronger than the silk that ladies sew with, yet by means of them the small people drew the boat along merrily. There were so many of them that they looked like an army as they marched in the light of the lanterns and torches. Jack thought they were very happy, though the work was hard, for they shouted and sang.

The fairy woman looked more beautiful than ever now, and far more stately. She had on a band of precious stones to bind back her hair, and they shone so brightly in the night that her features could be clearly seen.

Jack's little favorite was fast asleep, and the other two fairies had flown away. He was beginning to feel rather sleepy himself, when he was roused by the voice of his free lady, who said to him, "Jack, there is no one listening now, so I will tell you my story. I am the Fairy Queen!"

Jack opened his eyes very wide, but he was so much surprised that he did not say a word.

"One day, long, long ago," said the Queen, "I was discontented with my own happy country. I wished to see the world, so I set forth with a number of the one-foot-one fairies, and went down the wonderful river, thinking to see the world.

"So we sailed down the river till we came to that town which you know of; and there, in the very middle of the stream, stood a tower,—a tall tower, built upon a rock.

"Fairies are afraid of nothing but of other fairies, and we did not think this tower was fairy-work, so we left our ship and went up the 109 rock and into the tower, to see what it was like; but just as we had descended into the dungeon keep, we heard the gurgling of water overhead, and down came the tower. It was nothing but water enchanted into the likeness of stone, and we all fell down with it into the very bed of the river.

"Of course we were not drowned, but there we were obliged to lie, for we have no power out of our own element; and the next day the towns-people came down with a net and dragged the river, picked us all out of the meshes, and made us slaves. The one-foot-one fairies got away shortly; but from that day to this, in sorrow and distress, I have had to serve my masters. Luckily, my crown had fallen off in the water, so I was not known to be the Queen; but till you came, Jack, I had almost forgotten that I had ever been happy and free, and I had hardly any hope of getting away."

"How sorry your people must have been," 110 said Jack, "when they found you did not come home again."

"No," said the Queen: "they only went to sleep, and they will not wake till to-morrow morning, when I pass in again. They will think I have been absent for a day, and so will the apple-woman. You must not undeceive them; if you do, they will be very angry."

"And who is the apple-woman?" inquired Jack; but the Queen blushed, and pretended not to hear the question, so he repeated,—

"Queen, who is the apple-woman?"

"I've only had her for a very little while," said the Queen, evasively.

"And how long do you think you have been a slave, Queen?" asked Jack.

"I don't know," said the Queen. "I have never been able to make up my mind about that."

And now all the moons began to shine, and all the trees lighted themselves up, for almost every leaf had a glowworm or a fire-fly on it, 111 and the water was full of fishes that had shining eyes. And now they were close to the steep mountain side; and Jack looked and saw an opening in it, into which the river ran. It was a kind of cave, something like a long, long church with a vaulted roof, only the pavement of it was that magic river, and a narrow towing-path ran on either side.

As they entered the cave there was a hollow, murmuring sound, and the Queen's crown became so bright that it lighted up the whole boat; at the same time she began to tell Jack a wonderful story, which he liked very much to hear, but every fresh thing she said he forgot what had gone before; and at last, though he tried very hard to listen, he was obliged to go to sleep; and he slept soundly, and never dreamed of anything, till it was morning.

He saw such a curious sight when he woke! They had been going through this underground cavern all night, and now they were approaching its opening on the other side. This opening, 112 because they were a good way from it yet, looked like a lovely little round window of blue and yellow and green glass, but as they drew on he could see far-off mountains, blue sky, and a country all covered with sunshine.

He heard singing, too, such as fairies make; and he saw some beautiful people, such as those fairies whom he had brought with him. They were coming along the towing-path. They were all lady fairies; but they were not very polite, for as each one came up she took a silken rope out of a brown sailor's hand, and gave him a shove which pushed him into the water. In fact, the water became filled with such swarms of these sailors that the boat could hardly get on. But the poor little brown fellows did not seem to mind this conduct, for they plunged and shook themselves about, scattering a good deal of spray. Then they all suddenly dived, and when they came up again they were ducks,—nothing but brown ducks, I assure you, with green stripes on their wings; and with a great deal of quacking 113 and floundering, they all began to swim back again as fast as they could.

Then Jack was a good deal vexed, and he said to himself, "If nobody thanks the ducks for towing us I will"; so he stood up in the boat and shouted, "Thank you, ducks; we are very much obliged to you!" But neither the Queen nor these new towers took the least notice, and gradually the boat came out of that dim cave and entered Fairyland, while the river became so narrow that you could hear the song of the towers quite easily; those on the right bank sang the first verse, and those on the left bank answered:—

> Drop, drop from the leaves of lign aloes, O honey-dew! drop from the tree. Float up through your clear river shallows, White lilies, beloved of the bee.
>
> Let the people, O Queen! say, and bless thee, Her bounty drops soft as the dew, And spotless in honor confess thee, As lilies are spotless in hue.
>
> 114 On the roof stands yon white stork awaking, His feathers flush rosy the while, For, lo! from the blushing east breaking, The sun sheds the bloom of his smile.
>
> Let them boast of thy word, "It is certain; We doubt it no more," let them say, "Than tomorrow that night's dusky curtain Shall roll back its folds for the day."

"Master," whispered the old hound, who was lying at Jack's feet.

"Well," said Jack.

"They didn't invent that song themselves," said the hound; "the old apple-woman taught it to them,—the woman whom they love because she can make them cry."

Jack was rather ashamed of the hound's rudeness in saying this; but the Queen took no notice. And now they had reached a little landing-place, which ran out a few feet into the river, and was strewed thickly with cowslips and violets.

THE QUEEN.

"Here the boat stopped, and the Queen rose and got out."—.

Here the boat stopped, and the Queen rose and got out.

Jack watched her. A whole crowd of one-foot-one fairies came down a garden to meet her, and he saw them conduct her to a beautiful tent, with golden poles and a silken covering; but nobody took the slightest notice of him, or of little Mopsa, or of the hound, and after a long silence the hound said, "Well, master, don't you feel hungry? Why don't you go with the others and have some breakfast?"

"The Queen didn't invite me," said Jack.

"But do you feel as if you couldn't go?" asked the hound.

"Of course not," answered Jack; "but perhaps I may not."

"Oh, yes, master," replied the hound; "whatever you can do in Fairyland you may do."

"Are you sure of that?" asked Jack.

"Quite sure, master," said the hound; "and I am hungry too."

"Well," said Jack, "I will go there and take Mopsa. She shall ride on my shoulder; you may follow."

So he walked up that beautiful garden till he came to the great tent. A banquet was going on inside. All the one-foot-one fairies sat down the sides of the table, and at the top sat the Queen on a larger chair; and there were two empty chairs, one on each side of her.

Jack blushed; but the hound whispering again, "Master, whatever you can do you may do," he came slowly up the table towards the Queen, who was saying, as he drew near, "Where is our trusty and well-beloved, the apple-woman?" And she took no notice of Jack; so, though he could not help feeling rather red and ashamed, he went and sat in the chair beside her with Mopsa still on his shoulder. Mopsa laughed for joy when she saw the feast. The Queen said, "O Jack, I am so glad to see you!" and some of the one-foot-one fairies cried out, "What a delightful little creature that is! She can laugh! Perhaps she can also cry!"

Jack looked about, but there was no seat for 117 Mopsa; and he was afraid to let her run about on the floor, lest she should be hurt.

There was a very large dish standing before the Queen; for though the people were small, the plates and dishes were exactly like those we use, and of the same size.

This dish was raised on a foot, and filled with grapes and peaches. Jack wondered at himself for doing it, but he saw no other place for Mopsa; so he took out the fruit, laid it round the dish, and set his own little one-foot-one in the dish.

Nobody looked in the least surprised; and there she sat very happily, biting an apple with her small white teeth.

Then, as they brought him nothing to eat, Jack helped himself from some of the dishes before him, and found that a fairy breakfast was very nice indeed.

In the meantime there was a noise outside, and in stumped an elderly woman. She had very thick boots on, a short gown of red print, an 118 orange cotton handkerchief over her shoulders, and a black silk bonnet. She was exactly the same height as the Queen,—for of course nobody in Fairyland is allowed to be any bigger than the Queen; so, if they are not children when they arrive, they are obliged to shrink.

"How are you, dear?" said the Queen.

"I am as well as can be expected," answered the apple-woman, sitting down in the empty chair. "Now, then, where's my tea? They're never ready with my cup of tea."

Two attendants immediately brought a cup of tea, and set it down before the apple-woman, with a plate of bread and butter; and she proceeded to pour it into the saucer, and blow it, because it was hot. In so doing her wandering eyes caught sight of Jack and little Mopsa, and she set down the saucer, and looked at them with attention.

Now Mopsa, I am sorry to say, was behaving so badly that Jack was quite ashamed of her. First, she got out of her dish, took something 119 nice out of the Queen's plate with her fingers, and ate it; and then, as she was going back, she tumbled over a melon, and upset a glass of red wine, which she wiped up with her white frock; after which she got into her dish again, and there she sat smiling, and daubing her pretty face with a piece of buttered muffin.

"Mopsa," said Jack, "you are very naughty; if you behave in this way, I shall never take you out to parties again."

"Pretty lamb!" said the apple-woman; "It's just like a child." And then she burst into tears, and exclaimed, sobbing, "It's many a long day since I've seen a child. Oh dear! oh deary me!"

Upon this, to the astonishment of Jack, every one of the guests began to cry and sob too.

"Oh dear! oh dear!" they said to one another, "we're crying; we can cry just as well as men and women. Isn't it delightful? What a luxury it is to cry, to be sure!"

They were evidently quite proud of it; and 120 when Jack looked at the Queen for an explanation, she only gave him a still little smile.

But Mopsa crept along the table to the apple-woman, let her take her and hug her, and seemed to like her very much; for as she sat on her knee, she patted her brown face with a little dimpled hand.

"I should like vastly well to be her nurse," said the apple-woman, drying her eyes, and looking at Jack.

"If you'll always wash her, and put clean frocks on her, you may," said Jack; "for just look at her,—what a figure she is already!"

Upon this the apple-woman laughed for joy, and again every one else did the same. The fairies can only laugh and cry when they see mortals do so.

CHAPTER IX. AFTER THE PARTY.

Stephano.—This will prove a brave kingdom to me, Where I shall have my music for nothing.
The Tempest.

When breakfast was over, the guests got up, one after the other, without taking the least notice of the Queen; and the tent began to get so thin and transparent that you could see the trees and the sky through it. At last, it looked only like a colored mist, with blue, and green, and yellow stripes, and then it was gone; and the table and all the things on it began to go in the same way. Only Jack, and the apple-woman, and Mopsa were left, sitting on their chairs, with the Queen between them.

Presently, the Queen's lips began to move, and her eyes looked straight before her, as she sat upright in her chair. Whereupon the apple-woman snatched up Mopsa, and, seizing Jack's hand, hurried him off, exclaiming, "Come away! come away! She is going to tell one of her stories; and if you listen, you'll be obliged to go to sleep, and sleep nobody knows how long."

Jack did not want to go to sleep; he wished to go down to the river again, and see what had become of his boat, for he had left his cap and several other things in it.

So he parted from the apple-woman,—who took Mopsa with her, and said he would find her again when he wanted her at her apple-stall,—and went down to the boat, where he saw that his faithful hound was there before him.

"It was lucky, master, that I came when I did," said the hound, "for a dozen or so of those one-foot-one fellows were just shoving it off, and you will want it at night to sleep in."

"Yes," said Jack; "and I can stretch the bit of purple silk to make a canopy over head,—a sort of awning,—for I should not like to sleep in tents or palaces that are inclined to melt away."

So the hound with his teeth, and Jack with his hands, pulled and pulled at the silk till it was large enough to make a splendid canopy, like a tent; and it reached down to the water's edge, and roofed in all the after part of the boat.

So now he had a delightful little home of his own; and there was no fear of its being blown away, for no wind ever blows in Fairyland. All the trees are quite still, no leaf rustles, and the flowers lie on the ground exactly where they fall.

After this Jack told the hound to watch his boat, and went himself in search of the apple-woman. Not one fairy was to be seen, any more than if he had been in his own country, and he wandered down the green margin of the river till he saw the apple-woman sitting at a small stall with apples on it, and cherries tied to sticks, and some dry-looking nuts. She had Mopsa on her knee, and had washed her face, and put a beautiful clean white frock on her.

"Where are all the fairies gone to?" asked Jack.

"I never take any notice of that common trash and their doings," she answered. "When the Queen takes to telling her stories they are generally frightened, and go and sit in the tops of the trees."

"But you seem very fond of Mopsa," said Jack, "and she is one of them. You will help me to take care of her, won't you, tills she grows a little older?"

"Grows!" said the apple-woman, laughing. "Grows! Why you don't think, surely, that she will ever be any different from what she is now?"

"I thought she would grow up," said Jack.

"They never change so long as they last," 125 answered the apple-woman, "when once they are one-foot-one high."

"Mopsa," said Jack, "come here, and I'll measure you."

Mopsa came dancing towards Jack, and he tried to measure her, first with a yard measure that the apple-woman took out of her pocket, and then with a stick, and then with a bit of string; but Mopsa would not stand steady, and at last it ended in their having a good game of romps together, and a race; but when he carried her back, sitting on his shoulder, he was sorry to see that the apple-woman was crying again, and he asked her kindly what she did it for.

"It is because," she answered, "I shall never see my own country any more, nor any men and women and children, excepting such as by a rare chance stray in for a little while as you have done."

"I can go back whenever I please," said Jack. "Why don't you?"

"Because I came in of my own good-will, after I had had fair warning that if I came at all 126 it would end in my staying always. Besides, I don't know that I exactly wish to go home again: I should be afraid."

"Afraid of what?" asked Jack.

"Why, there's the rain and the cold, and not having anything to eat excepting what you earn. And yet," said the apple-woman, "I have three boys of my own at home; one of them must be nearly a man by this time, and the youngest is about as old as you are. If I went home I might find one or more of those boys in jail, and then how miserable I should be."

"But you are not happy as it is," said Jack. "I have seen you cry."

"Yes," said the apple-woman; "but now I live here I don't care about anything so much as I used to do. 'May I have a satin gown and a coach?' I asked, when first I came. 'You may have a hundred and fifty satin gowns if you like,' said the Queen, 'and twenty coaches with six cream-colored horses to each.' But when I had been here a little time, and found I could 127 have everything I wished for, and change it as often as I pleased, I began not to care for anything; and at last I got so sick of all their grand things that I dressed myself in my own clothes that I came in, and made up my mind to have a stall and sit at it, as I used to do, selling apples. And I used to say to myself, 'I have but to wish with all my heart to go home, and I can go, I know that;' but oh dear! oh dear! I couldn't wish enough, for it would come into my head that I should be poor, or that my boys would have forgotten me, or that my neighbors would look down on me, and so I always put off wishing for another day. Now here is the Queen coming. Sit down on the grass and play with Mopsa. Don't let her see us talking together, lest she should think I have been telling you things which you ought not to know."

Jack looked, and saw the Queen coming slowly towards them, with her hands held out before her, as if it was dark. She felt her way, yet her eyes were wide open, and she was telling her stories all the time.

"Don't you listen to a word she says," whispered the apple-woman; and then, in order that Jack might not hear what the Queen was talking about, she began to sing.

She had no sooner begun than up from the river came swarms of one-foot-one fairies to listen, and hundreds of them dropped down from the trees. The Queen, too, seemed to attend as they did, though she kept murmuring her story all the time; and nothing that any of them did appeared to surprise the apple-woman,—she sang as if nobody was taking any notice at all:—

When I sit on market-days amid the comers and the goers, Oh! full oft I have a vision of the days without alloy, And a ship comes up the river with a jolly gang of towers, And a "pull'e haul'e, pull'e haul'e, yoy! heave, hoy!"

There is busy talk around me, all about mine ears it hummeth, But the wooden wharves I look on, and a dancing, heaving buoy, For 'tis tidetime in the river, and she cometh—oh, she cometh! With a "pull'e haul'e, pull'e haul'e, yoy! heave, hoy!"

129 Then I hear the water washing, never golden waves were brighter, And I hear the capstan creaking—'tis a sound that cannot cloy. Bring her to, to ship her lading, brig or schooner, sloop or lighter, With a "pull'e haul'e, pull'e haule, yoy! heave, hoy!"

"Will ye step aboard, my dearest? for the high seas lie before us." So I sailed adown the river in those days without alloy. We are launched! But when, I wonder, shall a sweeter sound float o'er us Than yon "pull'e haul'e, pull'e haul'e, yoy! heave, hoy!"

As the apple-woman left off singing, the Queen moved away, still murmuring the words of her story, and Jack said,—

"Does the Queen tell stories of what has happened, or of what is going to happen?"

"Why, of what is going to happen, of course," replied the woman. "Anybody could tell the other sort."

"Because I heard a little of it," observed Jack. "I thought she was talking of me. She said 130 'So he took the measure, and Mopsa stood still for once, and he found she was only one foot high, and she grew a great deal after that. Yes, she can grow.'"

"That's a fine hearing, and a strange hearing," said the apple-woman; "and what did she mutter next?"

"Of how she heard me sobbing," replied Jack; "and while you went on about stepping on board the ship, she said, 'He was very good to me, dear little fellow! But Fate is the name of my old mother, and she reigns here. Oh, she reigns! The fatal F is in her name, and I cannot take it out!'"

"Ah!" replied the apple-woman, "they all say that, and that they are fays, and that mortals call their history fable; they are always crying out for an alphabet without the fatal F."

"And then she told how she heard Mopsa sobbing too," said Jack; "sobbing among the reeds and rushes by the river side."

"There are no reeds, and no rushes either, 131 here," said the apple-woman, "and I have walked the river from end to end. I don't think much of that part of the story. But you are sure she said that Mopsa was short of her proper height?"

"Yes, and that she would grow; but that's nothing. In my country we always grow."

"Hold your tongue about you country!" said the apple-woman, sharply. "Do you want to make enemies of them all?"

Mopsa had been listening to this, and now she said, "I don't love the Queen. She slapped my arm as she went by, and it hurts."

Mopsa showed her little fat arm as she spoke, and there was a red place on it.

"That's odd, too," said the apple-woman; "there's nothing red in a common fairy's veins. They have sap in them: that's why they can't blush."

Just then the sun went down, and Mopsa got up on the apple-woman's lap, and went to sleep; and Jack, being tired, went to his boat and lay down under the purple canopy, his old hound lying at his feet to keep guard over him.

The next morning, when he woke, a pretty voice called to him, "Jack! Jack!" and he opened his eyes and saw Mopsa. The apple-woman had dressed her in a clean frock and blue shoes, and her hair was so long! She was standing on the landing-place, close to him. "O Jack! I'm so big," she said. "I grew in the night; look at me."

Jack looked. Yes, Mopsa had grown indeed; she had only just reached to his knee the day before, and now her little bright head, when he measured her, came as high as the second button of his waistcoat.

"But I hope you will not go on growing so fast as this," said Jack, "or you will be as tall as my mamma is in a week or two,—much too big for me to play with."

CHAPTER X. MOPSA LEARNS HER LETTERS.

A——apple-pie. B——bit it.

"How ashamed I am," Jack said, "to think that you don't know even your letters!"

Mopsa replied that she thought that did not signify, and then she and Jack began to play at jumping from the boat on to the bank, and back again; and afterwards, as not a single fairy could be seen, they had breakfast with the apple-woman.

"Where is the Queen?" asked Jack.

The apple-woman answered, "It's not the fashion to ask questions in Fairyland."

"That's a pity," said Jack, "for there are several 134 things that I particularly want to know about this country. Mayn't I even ask how big it is?"

"How big?" said Mopsa,—little Mopsa looking as wise as possible. "Why, the same size as your world, of course."

Jack laughed. "It's the same world that you call yours," continued Mopsa; "and when I'm a little older, I'll explain it all to you."

"If it's our world," said Jack, "why are none of us in it, excepting me and the apple-woman?"

"That's because you've got something in your world that you call Time," said Mopsa; "so you talk about NOW, and you talk about THEN."

"And don't you?" asked Jack.

"I do if I want to make you understand," said Mopsa.

The apple-woman laughed, and said, "To think of the pretty thing talking so queen-like already! Yes, that's right, and just what the grown-up fairies say. Go on, and explain it to him if you can."

"You know," said Mopsa, "that your people 135 say there was a time when there were none of them in the world,—a time before they were made. Well, THIS is that time. This is long ago."

"Nonsense!" said Jack. "Then how do I happen to be here?"

"Because," said Mopsa, "when the albatross brought you, she did not fly with you a long way off, but a long way back,—hundreds and hundreds of years. This is your world, as you can see; but none of your people are here, because they are not made yet. I don't think any of them will be made for a thousand years."

"But I saw the old ships," answered Jack, "in the enchanted bay."

"That was a border country," said Mopsa. "I was asleep while you went through those countries; but these are the real Fairylands."

Jack was very much surprised when he heard Mopsa say these strange things; and as he looked at her, he felt that a sleep was coming over him, and he could not hold up his head. He 136 felt how delightful it was to go to sleep; and though the apple-woman sprang to him, when she observed that he was shutting his eyes, and though he heard her begging and entreating him to keep awake, he did not want to do so; but he let his head sink down on the mossy grass, which was as soft as a pillow, and there, under the shade of a Guelder rose-tree, that kept dropping its white flowerets all over him, he had this dream:

He thought that Mopsa came running up to him, as he stood by the river, and that he said to her, "Oh, Mopsa, how old we are! We have lived back to the times before Adam and Eve!"

"Yes," said Mopsa; "but I don't feel old. Let us go down the river, and see what we can find."

So they got into the boat, and it floated into the middle of the river, and then made for the opposite bank, where the water was warm and very muddy, and the river became so very wide that it seemed to be afternoon when they got 137 near enough to see it clearly; and what they saw was a boggy country, green, and full of little rills; but the water,—which, as I told you, was thick and muddy,—the water was full of small holes! You never saw water with eyelet-holes in it; but Jack did. On all sides of the boat he saw holes moving about in pairs, and some were so close that he looked and saw their lining: they were lined with pink, and they snorted! Jack was afraid, but he considered that this was such a long time ago that the holes, whatever they were, could not hurt him; but it made him start, notwithstanding, when a huge flat-head reared itself up close to the boat, and he found that the holes were the nostrils of creatures who kept all the rest of themselves under water.

In a minute or two, hundreds of ugly flat-heads popped up, and the boat danced among them as they floundered about in the water.

"I hope they won't upset us," said Jack. "I wish you would land."

Mopsa said she would rather not, because she did not like the hairy elephants.

"There are no such things as hairy elephants," said Jack, in his dream; but he had hardly spoken when out of a wood close at hand some huge creatures, far larger than our elephants, came jogging down to the water. There were forty or fifty of them, and they were covered with what looked like tow. In fact, so coarse was their shaggy hair that they looked as if they were dressed in door-mats; and when they stood still and shook themselves, such clouds of dust flew out that, as it swept over the river, it almost stifled Jack and Mopsa.

"Odious!" exclaimed Jack, sneezing. "What terrible creatures these are!"

"Well," answered Mopsa, at the other end of the boat (but he could hardly see her for the dust), "then why do you dream of them?"

Jack had just decided to dream of something else, when, with a noise greater than fifty trumpets, the elephants, having shaken out all the dust, 139 came thundering down to the water to bathe in the liquid mud. They shook the whole country as they plunged; but that was not all. The awful river-horses rose up, and, with shrill screams, fell upon them, and gave them battle; while up from every rill peeped above the rushes frogs as large as oxen, and with blue and green eyes that gleamed like the eyes of cats.

The frogs croaking, and the shrill trumpeting of the elephants, together with the cries of the river-horses, as all these creatures fought with horn and tusk, and fell on one another, lashing the water into whirlpools, among which the boat danced up and down like a cork,—the blinding spray, and the flapping about of great bats over the boat and in it,—so confused Jack, that Mopsa had spoken to him several times before he answered.

"O Jack!" she said, at last; "if you can't dream any better, I must call the Craken."

"Very well," said Jack. "I'm almost wrapped 140 up and smothered in bats' wings, so call anything you please."

Thereupon Mopsa whistled softly, and in a minute or two he saw, almost spanning the river, a hundred yards off, a thing like a rainbow, or a slender bridge, or still more, like one ring or coil of an enormous serpent; and presently the creature's head shot up like a fountain, close to the boat, almost as high as a ship's mast. It was the Craken; and when Mopsa saw it, she began to cry, and said, "We are caught in this crowd of creatures, and we cannot get away from the land of dreams. Do help us, Craken!"

Some of the bats that hung to the edges of the boat had wings as large as sails; and the first thing the Craken did was to stoop its lithe neck, pick two or three of them off, and eat them.

"You can swim your boat home under my coils where the water is calm," the Craken said, "for she is so extremely old now, that if you do not take care she will drop to pieces before you get back to the present time."

Jack knew it was of no use saying anything to this formidable creature, before whom the river-horses and the elephants were rushing to the shore; but when he looked and saw down the river rainbow behind rainbow,—I mean coil behind coil,—glittering in the sun, like so many glorious arches that did not reach to the banks, he felt extremely glad that this was a dream, and besides that, he thought to himself, "It's only a fabled monster."

"No, it's only a fable to these times," said Mopsa, answering his thought; "but in spite of that we shall have to go through all the rings."

They went under one,—silver, green, and blue, and gold. The water dripped from it upon them, and the boat trembled, either because of its great age, or because it felt the rest of the coil underneath.

A good way off was another coil, and they went so safely under that, that Jack felt himself getting used to Crakens, and not afraid. 142 Then they went under thirteen more. These kept getting nearer and nearer together, but, besides that, the fourteenth had not quite such a high span as the former ones; but there were a great many to come, and yet they got lower and lower.

Both Jack and Mopsa noticed this, but neither said a word. The thirtieth coil brushed Jack's cap off, then they had to stoop to pass under the two next, and then they had to lie down in the bottom of the boat, and they got through with the greatest difficulty; but still before them was another! The boat was driving straight towards it, and it lay so close to the water that the arch it made was only a foot high. When Jack saw it, he called out, "No! that I cannot bear. Somebody else may do the rest of this dream. I shall jump overboard."

Mopsa seemed to answer in quite a pleasant voice, as if she was not afraid,—

"No, you'd much better wake." And then she went on, "Jack! Jack! why don't you wake!"

Then all on a sudden Jack opened his eyes, and found that he was lying quietly on the grass, that little Mopsa really had asked him why he did not wake. He saw the Queen too, standing by, looking at him, and saying to herself, "I did not put him to sleep. I did not put him to sleep."

"We don't want any more stories to-day, Queen," said the apple-woman, in a disrespectful tone, and she immediately began to sing, clattering some tea-things all the time, for a kettle was boiling on some sticks, and she was going to make tea out of doors:—

The marten flew to the finch's nest, Feathers, and moss, and a wisp of hay: "The arrow it sped to thy brown mate's breast; Low in the broom is thy mate to-day."

"Liest thou low, love? low in the broom? Feathers and moss, and a wisp of hay, Warm the white eggs till I learn his doom." She beateth her wings, and away, away.

"Ah, my sweet singer, thy days are told (Feathers and moss, and a wisp of hay)! Thine eyes are dim, and the eggs grow cold. O mournful morrow! O dark to-day!"

The finch flew back to her cold, cold nest, Feathers and moss, and a wisp of hay, Mine is the trouble that rent her breast, And home is silent, and love is clay.

Jack felt very tired indeed,—as much tired as if he had really been out all day on the river, and gliding under the coils of the Craken. He however rose up, when the apple-woman called him, and drank his tea, and had some fairy bread with it, which refreshed him very much.

After tea he measured Mopsa again, and found that she had grown up to a higher button. She looked much wiser too, and when he said she must be taught to read she made no objection, so he arranged daisies and buttercups into the forms of the letters, and she learnt nearly all of them that one evening, while crowds of the one-foot-one fairies looked on, hanging from the boughs and sitting in the grass, and shouting out 145 the names of the letters as Mopsa said them. They were very polite to Jack, for they gathered all these flowers for him, and emptied them from their little caps at his feet as fast as he wanted them.

CHAPTER XI. GOOD-MORNING, SISTER.

Sweet is childhood—childhood's over, Kiss and part. Sweet is youth; but youth's a rover—
So's my heart. Sweet is rest; but by all showing Toil is nigh. We must go. Alas! the going, Say
"good-bye."

Jack crept under his canopy, went to sleep early that night, and did not wake till the sun had risen, when the apple-woman called him, and said breakfast was nearly ready.

The same thing never happens twice in Fairyland, so this time the breakfast was not spread in a tent, but on the river. The Queen had cut off a tiny piece of her robe, the one-foot-one fairies had stretched it till it was very large, and 147 then they had spread it on the water, where it floated and lay like a great carpet of purple and gold. One corner of it was moored to the side of Jack's boat; but he had not observed this, because of his canopy. However, that was now looped up by the apple-woman, and Jack and Mopsa saw what was going on.

Hundreds of swans had been towing the carpet along, and were still holding it with their beaks, while a crowd of doves walked about on it, smoothing out the creases and patting it with their pretty pink feet till it was quite firm and straight. The swans then swam away, and they flew away.

Presently troops of fairies came down to the landing-place, jumped into Jack's boat without asking leave, and so got on to the carpet, while at the same time a great tree which grew on the bank began to push out fresh leaves, as large as fans, and shoot out long branches, which again shot out others, till very soon there was shade all over the carpet,—a thick shadow as good as 148 a tent, which was very pleasant, for the sun was already hot.

When the Queen came down, the tree suddenly blossomed out with thousands of red and white flowers.

"You must not go on to that carpet," said the apple-woman; "let us sit still in the boat, and be served here." She whispered this as the Queen stepped into the boat.

"Good-morning, Jack," said the Queen. "Good-morning, dear." This was to the apple-woman; and then she stood still for a moment and looked earnestly at little Mopsa, and sighed.

"Well," she said to her, "don't you mean to speak to me?" Then Mopsa lifted up her pretty face and blushed very rosy red, and said, in a shy voice, "Good morning——sister."

"I said so!" exclaimed the Queen; "I said so!" and she lifted up her beautiful eyes, and murmured out, "What is to be done now?"

"Never mind, Queen dear," said Jack. "If it was rude of Mopsa to say that, she is such a 149 little young thing that she does not know better."

"It was not rude," said Mopsa, and she laughed and blushed again. "It was not rude, and I am not sorry."

As she said this the Queen stepped on to the carpet, and all the flowers began to drop down. They were something like camellias, and there were thousands of them.

The fairies collected them in little heaps. They had no tables and chairs, nor any plates and dishes for this breakfast; but the Queen sat down on the carpet close to Jack's boat, and leaned her cheek on her hand, and seemed to be lost in thought. The fairies put some flowers into her lap, then each took some, and they all sat down and looked at the Queen, but she did not stir.

At last Jack said, "When is the breakfast coming?"

"This is the breakfast," said the apple-woman; "these flowers are most delicious eating. You never tasted anything so good in your life; but we don't begin till the Queen does."

Quantities of blossoms had dropped into the boat. Several fairies tumbled into it almost head over heels, they were in such a hurry, and they heaped them into Mopsa's lap, but took no notice of Jack, nor of the apple-woman either.

At last, when every one had waited some time, the Queen pulled a petal off one flower, and began to eat, so every one else began; and what the apple-woman had said was quite true. Jack knew that he never had tasted anything half so nice, and he was quite sorry when he could not eat any more. So, when every one had finished, the Queen leaned her arm on the edge of the boat, and, turning her lovely face towards Mopsa, said, "I want to whisper to you, sister."

"Oh!" said Mopsa, "I wish I was in Jack's waistcoat pocket again; but I'm so big now." And she took hold of the two sides of his velvet jacket, and hid her face between them.

"My old mother sent a message last night," continued the Queen, in a soft, sorrowful voice. "She is much more powerful than we are."

"What is the message?" asked Mopsa; but she still hid her face.

So the Queen moved over, and put her lips close to Mopsa's ear, and repeated it: "There cannot be two Queens in one hive."

"If Mopsa leaves the hive, a fine swarm will go with her," said the apple-woman. "I shall, for one; that I shall!"

"No!" answered the Queen. "I hope not, dear; for you know well that this is my old mother's doing, not mine."

"Oh!" said Mopsa; "I feel as if I must tell a story too, just as the Queen does." But the apple-woman broke out in a very cross voice, "It's not at all like Fairyland, if you go on in this way, and I would as lieve be out of it as in it." Then she began to sing, that she and Jack might not hear Mopsa's story:—

On the rocks by Aberdeen, Where the whislin' wave had been, As I wandered and at e'en Was eerie; There I saw thee sailing west, And I ran with joy opprest— Ay, and took out all my best, My dearie.

Then I busked mysel' wi' speed, And the neighbors cried "What need? 'Tis a lass in any weed Aye bonny!" Now my heart, my heart is sair. What's the good, though I be fair, For thou'lt never see me mair, Man Johnnie!

While the apple-woman sang Mopsa finished her story; and the Queen untied the fastening which held her carpet to the boat, and went floating upon it down the river.

"Good-by," she said, kissing her hand to them. "I must go and prepare for the deputation."

So Jack and Mopsa played about all the morning, sometimes in the boat and sometimes on the shore, while the apple-woman sat on the grass, with her arms folded, and seemed to be lost in thought. At last she said to Jack, "What was the name of the great bird that carried you two here?"

"I have forgotten," answered Jack. "I've been trying to remember ever since we heard the Queen tell her first story, but I cannot."

"I remember," said Mopsa.

"Tell it then," replied the apple-woman; but Mopsa shook her head.

"I don't want Jack to go," she answered.

"I don't want to go, nor that you should," said Jack.

"But the Queen said, 'there cannot be two queens in one hive,' and that means that you are going to be turned out of this beautiful country."

"The other fairy lands are just as nice," answered Mopsa; "she can only turn me out of this one."

"I never heard of more than one Fairyland," observed Jack.

"It's my opinion," said the apple-woman, "that there are hundreds! And those one-foot-one fairies are such a saucy set, that if I were you I should be very glad to get away from them. You've been here a very little while as yet, and you've no notion what goes on when the leaves begin to drop."

"Tell us," said Jack.

"Well, you must know," answered the apple-woman, "that fairies cannot abide cold weather; so, when the first rime frost comes, they bury themselves."

"Bury themselves?" repeated Jack.

"Yes, I tell you, they bury themselves. You've seen fairy rings, of course, even in your own country; and here the fields are full of them. Well, when it gets cold, a company of fairies forms itself into a circle, and every one digs a little hole. The first that has finished jumps into his hole, and his next neighbor covers him up, 155 and then jumps into his own little hole, and he gets covered up in his turn, till at last there is only one left, and he goes and joins another circle, hoping he shall have better luck than to be last again. I've often asked them why they do that, but no fairy can ever give a reason for anything. They always say that old Mother Fate makes them do it. When they come up again, they are not fairies at all, but the good ones are mushrooms, and the bad ones are toadstools."

"Then you think there are no one-foot-one fairies in the other countries," said Jack.

"Of course not," answered the apple-woman; "all the fairy lands are different. It's only the queens that are alike."

"I wish the fairies would not disappear for hours," said Jack. "They all seem to run off and hide themselves."

"That's their way," answered the apple-woman. "All fairies are part of their time in the shape 156 of human creatures, and the rest of it in the shape of some animal. These can turn themselves, when they please, into Guinea-fowl. In the heat of the day they generally prefer to be in that form, and they sit among the leaves of the trees.

THE APPLE WOMAN.

"So she began to sing."—.

"A great many are now with the Queen, because there is a deputation coming; but if I were to begin to sing, such a flock of Guinea-hens would gather round, that the boughs of the trees would bend with their weight, and they would light on the grass all about so thickly that not a blade of grass would be seen as far as the song was heard."

So she began to sing, and the air was darkened by great flocks of these Guinea-fowl. They alighted just as she had said, and kept time with their heads and their feet, nodding like a crowd of mandarins; and yet it was nothing but a stupid old song that you would have thought could have no particular meaning for them.

CHAPTER XII. THEY RUN AWAY FROM OLD MOTHER FATE.

A land that living warmth disowns, It meets my wondering ken; A land where all the men are stones, Or all the stones are men.

Before the apple-woman had finished, Jack and Mopsa saw the Queen coming in great state, followed by thousands of the one-foot-one fairies, and leading by a ribbon round its neck a beautiful brown doe. A great many pretty fawns were walking among the fairies.

"Here's the deputation," said the apple-woman; but as the Guinea-fowl rose like a cloud at the approach of the Queen, and the fairies and fawns pressed forward, there was a good deal of noise and confusion, during which Mopsa stepped up close to Jack, and whispered in his ear, "Remember, Jack, whatever you can do you may do."

Then the brown doe laid down at Mopsa's feet, and the Queen began:—

"Jack and Mopsa, I love you both. I had a message last night from my old mother, and I told you what it was."

"Yes, Queen," said Mopsa, "you did."

"And now," continued the Queen, "she has sent this beautiful brown doe from the country beyond the lake, where they are in the greatest distress for a queen, to offer Mopsa the crown; and, Jack, it is fated that Mopsa is to reign there, so you had better say no more about it."

"I don't want to be a queen," said Mopsa, pouting; "I want to play with Jack."

"You are a queen already," answered the real Queen; "at least, you will be in a few days. You are so much grown, even since the morning, that you come up nearly to Jack's shoulder. In four days you will be as tall as I am; and it is quite impossible that any one of fairy birth should be as tall as a queen in her own country."

"But I don't see what stags and does can want with a queen," said Jack.

"They were obliged to turn into deer," said the Queen, "when they crossed their own border; but they are fairies when they are at home, and they want Mopsa, because they are always obliged to have a queen of alien birth."

"If I go," said Mopsa, "shall Jack go too?"

"Oh, no," answered the Queen; "Jack and the apple-woman are my subjects."

"Apple-woman," said Jack, "tell us what you think; shall Mopsa go to this country?"

"Why, child," said the apple-woman, "go away from here she must; but she need not go off with the deer, I suppose, unless she likes. They look gentle and harmless; but it is very hard to get at the truth in this country, and I've heard queer stories about them."

"Have you?" said the Queen. "Well, you can repeat them if you like; but remember that the poor brown doe cannot contradict them."

So the apple-woman said, "I have heard, but I don't know how true it is, that in that country they shut up their queen in a great castle, and cover her with a veil, and never let the sun shine on her; for if by chance the least little sunbeam should light on her she would turn into a doe directly, and all the nation would turn with her, and stay so."

"I don't want to be shut up in a castle," said Mopsa.

"But is it true?" asked Jack.

"Well," said the apple-woman, "as I told you before, I cannot make out whether it's true or not, for all these stags and fawns look very mild, gentle creatures."

"I won't go," said Mopsa; "I would rather run away."

All this time the Queen with the brown doe had been gently pressing with the crowd nearer and nearer to the brink of the river, so that now 162 Jack and Mopsa, who stood facing them, were quite close to the boat; and while they argued and tried to make Mopsa come away, Jack suddenly whispered to her to spring into the boat, which she did, and he after her, and at the same time he cried out,—

"Now, boat, if you are my boat, set off as fast as you can, and let nothing of fairy birth get on board of you."

No sooner did he begin to speak than the boat swung itself away from the edge, and almost in a moment it was in the very middle of the river, and beginning to float gently down with the stream.

THEY RUN AWAY FROM OLD MOTHER FATE.

"The boat swung itself away from the edge, and almost in a moment it was in the very middle of the river."—.

Now, as I have told you before, that river runs up the country instead of down to the sea, so Jack and Mopsa floated still farther up into Fairyland; and they saw the Queen, and the apple-woman, and all the crowd of fawns and fairies walking along the bank of the river, keeping exactly to the same pace that the boat went; and this went on for hours and hours, so that 163 there seemed to be no chance that Jack and Mopsa could land; and they heard no voices at all, nor any sound but the baying of the old hound, who could not swim out to them, because Jack had forbidden the boat to take anything of fairy birth on board of her.

Luckily the bottom of the boat was full of those delicious flowers that had dropped into it at breakfast-time, so there was plenty of nice food for Jack and Mopsa; and Jack noticed, when he looked at her towards evening, that she was now nearly as tall as himself, and that her lovely brown hair floated down to her ankles.

"Jack," she said, before it grew dusk, "will you give me your little purse that has the silver fourpence in it?"

Now Mopsa had often played with this purse. It was lined with a nice piece of pale green silk, and when Jack gave it to her she pulled the silk out, and shook it, and patted it, and stretched it, just as the Queen had done, and it came into a most lovely cloak, which she tied round her 164 neck. Then she twisted up her long hair into a coil, and fastened it round her head, and called to the fire-flies which were beginning to glitter on the trees to come, and they came and alighted in a row upon the coil, and turned into diamonds directly. So now Mopsa had got a crown and a robe, and she was so beautiful that Jack thought he should never be tired of looking at her; but it was nearly dark now, and he was so sleepy and tired that he could not keep his eyes open, though he tried very hard, and he began to blink, and then he began to nod, and at last he fell fast asleep, and did not awake till the morning.

Then he sat up in the boat, and looked about him. A wonderful country, indeed!—no trees, no grass, no houses, nothing but red stones and red sand,—and Mopsa was gone. Jack jumped on shore, for the boat had stopped, and was close to the brink of the river. He looked about for some time, and at last, in the shadow of a pale brown rock, he found her; and oh! delightful 165 surprise, the apple-woman was there too. She was saying, "O my bones! Dearie, dearie me, how they do ache!" That was not surprising, for she had been out all night. She had walked beside the river with the Queen and her tribe till they came to a little tinkling stream, which divides their country from the sandy land, and there they were obliged to stop; they could not cross it. But the apple-woman sprang over, and, though the Queen told her she must come back again in twenty-four hours, she did not appear to be displeased. Now the Guinea-hens, when they had come to listen, the day before, to the apple-woman's song, had brought each of them a grain of maize in her beak, and had thrown it into her apron; so when she got up she carried it with her gathered up there, and now she had been baking some delicious little cakes on a fire of dry sticks that the river had drifted down, and Mopsa had taken a honeycomb from the rock, so that they all had a very nice breakfast. And the apple-woman gave them a great deal 166 of good advice, and told them if they wished to remain in Fairyland, and not be caught by the brown doe and her followers, they must cross over the purple mountains. "For on the other side of those peaks," she said, "I have heard that fairies live who have the best of characters for being kind and just. I am sure they would never shut up a poor queen in a castle.

"But the best thing you could do, dear," she said to Mopsa, "would be to let Jack call the bird, and make her carry you back to his own country."

"The Queen is not at all kind," said Jack; "I have been very kind to her, and she should have let Mopsa stay."

"No, Jack, she could not," said Mopsa; "but I wish I had not grown so fast, and I don't like to go to your country. I would rather run away."

"But who is to tell us where to run?" asked Jack.

"Oh," said Mopsa, "some of these people."

"I don't see anybody," said Jack, looking about him.

Mopsa pointed to a group of stones, and then to another group, and as Jack looked he saw that in shape they were something like people,—stone people. One stone was a little like an old man with a mantle over him, and he was sitting on the ground with his knees up nearly to his chin. Another was like a woman with a hood on, and she seemed to be leaning her chin on her hand. Close to these stood something very much like a cradle in shape; and beyond were stones that resembled a flock of sheep lying down on the bare sand, with something that reminded Jack of the figure of a man lying asleep near them, with his face to the ground.

That was a very curious country; all the stones reminded you of people or of animals, and the shadows that they cast were much more like than the stones themselves. There were blocks with things that you might have mistaken for stone ropes twisted round them; but, looking at the shadows, you could see distinctly that they were trees, and that what coiled round were 168 snakes. Then there was a rocky prominence, at one side of which was something like a sitting figure, but its shadow, lying on the ground, was that of a girl with a distaff. Jack was very much surprised at all this; Mopsa was not. She did not see, she said, that one thing was more wonderful than another. All the fairy lands were wonderful, but the men-and-women world was far more so. She and Jack went about among the stones all day, and as the sun got low both the shadows and the blocks themselves became more and more like people, and if you went close you could now see features, very sweet, quiet features, but the eyes were all shut.

By this time the apple-woman began to feel very sad. She knew she should soon have to leave Jack and Mopsa, and she said to Mopsa, as they finished their evening meal, "I wish you would ask the inhabitants a few questions, dear, before I go, for I want to know whether they can put you in the way how to cross the purple mountains."

Jack said nothing, for he thought he would see what Mopsa was going to do; so when she got up and went towards the shape that was like a cradle he followed, and the apple-woman too. Mopsa went to the figure that sat by the cradle. It was a stone yet, but when Mopsa laid her little warm hand on its bosom it smiled.

"Dear," said Mopsa, "I wish you would wake."

A curious little sound was now heard, but the figure did not move, and the apple-woman lifted Mopsa on to the lap of the statue; then she put her arms round its neck, and spoke to it again very distinctly: "Dear! why don't you wake? You had better wake now; the baby's crying."

Jack now observed that the sound he had heard was something like the crying of a baby. He also heard the figure answering Mopsa. It said, "I am only a stone!"

"Then," said Mopsa, "I am not a queen yet. I cannot wake her. Take me down."

"I am not warm," said the figure; and that was quite true, and yet she was not a stone now which reminded one of a woman, but a woman that reminded one of a stone.

All the west was very red with the sunset, and the river was red too, and Jack distinctly saw some of the coils of rope glide down from the trees and slip into the water; next he saw the stones that had looked like sheep raise up their heads in the twilight, and then lift themselves and shake their woolly sides. At that instant the large white moon heaved up her pale face between two dark blue hills, and upon this the statue put out its feet and gently rocked the cradle.

Then it spoke again to Mopsa: "What was it that you wished me to tell you?"

"How to find the way over those purple mountains," said Mopsa.

"You must set off in an hour, then," said the woman; and she had hardly anything of the stone about her now. "You can easily find it by night 171 without any guide, but nothing can ever take you to it by day."

"But we would rather stay a few days in this curious country," said Jack; "let us wait at least till to-morrow night."

The statue at this moment rubbed her hands together, as if they still felt cold and stiff. "You are quite welcome to stay," she observed; "but you had better not."

"Why not?" persisted Jack.

"Father," said the woman, rising and shaking the figure next to her by the sleeve, "Wake up!" What had looked like an old man was a real old man now, and he got up and began to gather sticks to make a fire, and to pick up the little brown stones which had been scattered about all day, but which now were berries of coffee; the larger ones, which you might find here and there, were rasped rolls. Then the woman answered Jack, "Why not? Why, because it's full moon tonight at midnight, and the moment the moon is past the full your Queen, whose country 172 you have just left, will be able to cross over the little stream, and she will want to take you and that other mortal back. She can do it, of course, if she pleases; and we can afford you no protection, for by that time we shall be stones again. We are only people two hours out of the twenty-four."

"That is very hard," observed Jack.

"No," said the woman, in a tone of indifference; "it comes to the same thing, as we live twelve times as long as others do."

By this time the shepherd was gently driving his flock down to the water, and round fifty little fires groups of people were sitting roasting coffee, while cows were lowing to be milked, and girls with distaffs were coming to them slowly, for no one was in a hurry there. They say in that country that they wish to enjoy their day quietly, because it is so short.

"Can you tell us anything of the land beyond the mountains?" asked Jack.

"Yes," said the woman. "Of all fairy lands 173 it is the best; the people are the gentlest and kindest."

"Then I had better take Mopsa there than down the river?" said Jack.

"You can't take her down the river," replied the woman; and Jack thought she laughed and was glad of that.

"Why not?" asked Jack. "I have a boat."

"Yes, sir," answered the woman; "but where is it now?"

CHAPTER XIII. MELON SEEDS.

"Where is it now?" said the stone-woman; and when Jack heard that he ran down to the river, and looked right and looked left. At last he saw his boat,—a mere speck in the distance, it had floated so far.

He called it, but it was far beyond the reach of his voice; and Mopsa, who had followed him, said,—

"It does not signify, Jack, for I feel that no place is the right place for me but that country beyond the purple mountains, and I shall never be happy unless we go there."

So they walked back towards the stone-people hand in hand, and the apple-woman presently joined them. She was crying gently, for she knew that she must soon pass over the little stream, and part with these whom she called her dear children. Jack had often spoken to her that day about going home to her own country, but she said it was too late to think of that now, and she must end her days in the land of Faery.

The kind stone-people asked them to come and sit by their little fire; and in the dusk the woman whose baby had slept in a stone cradle took it up and began to sing to it. She seemed astonished when she heard that the apple-woman had power to go home if she could make up her mind to do it; and as she sang she looked at her with wonder and pity.

Little babe, while burns the west, Warm thee, warm thee in my breast; While the moon doth shine her best, And the dews distil not.

All the land so sad, so fair— Sweet its toils are, blest its care. Child, we may not enter there! Some there are that will not.

Fain would I thy margins know, Land of work, and land of snow; Land of life, whose rivers flow On, and on, and stay not.

Fain would I thy small limbs fold, While the weary hours are told, Little babe in cradle cold. Some there are that may not.

"You are not exactly fairies, I suppose?" said Jack. "If you were, you could go to our country when you pleased."

"No," said the woman; "we are not exactly fairies; but we shall be more like them when our punishment is over."

"I am sorry you are punished," answered Jack, "for you seem very nice, kind people."

"We were not always kind," answered the woman; "and perhaps we are only kind now because we have no time, and no chance of being otherwise. I'm sure I don't know about that. We were powerful once, and we did a cruel deed. I must not tell you what it was. We were told that our hearts were all as cold as stones,—and I suppose they were,—and we were doomed to be stones all our lives, excepting for the two hours of twilight. There was no one to sow the crops, or water the grass, so it all failed, and the trees died, and our houses fell, and our possessions were stolen from us."

"It is a very sad thing," observed the apple-woman; and then she said that she must go, for she had a long way to walk before she should reach the little brook that led to the country of her own queen; so she kissed the two children, Jack and Mopsa, and they begged her again to think better of it, and return to her own land. But she said No; she had no heart for work now, and could not bear either cold or poverty.

Then the woman who was hugging her little baby, and keeping it cosy and warm, began to tell Jack and Mopsa that it was time they should begin to run away to the country over the purple 178 mountains, or else the Queen would overtake them and be very angry with them; so, with many promises that they would mind her directions, they set off hand in hand to run; but before they left her they could see plainly that she was beginning to turn again into stone. However, she had given them a slice of melon with the seeds in it. It had been growing on the edge of the river, and was stone in the day-time, like everything else. "When you are tired," she said, "eat the seeds, and they will enable you to go running on. You can put the slice into this little red pot, which has string handles to it, and you can hang it on your arm. While you have it with you it will not turn to stone, but if you lay it down it will, and then it will be useless."

So, as I said before, Jack and Mopsa set off hand in hand to run; and as they ran all the things and people gradually and softly settled themselves to turn into stone again. Their cloaks and gowns left off fluttering, and hung stiffly; 179 and then they left off their occupations, and sat down, or laid down themselves; and the sheep and cattle turned stiff and stone-like too, so that in a very little while all that country was nothing but red stones and red sand, just as it had been in the morning.

Presently the full moon, which had been hiding behind a cloud, came out, and they saw their shadows, which fell straight before them; so they ran on hand in hand very merrily till the half-moon came up, and the shadows she made them cast fell sideways. This was rather awkward, because as long as only the full moon gave them shadows, they had but to follow them, in order to go straight towards the purple mountains. Now they were not always sure which were her shadows: and presently a crescent moon came, and still further confused them; also the sand began to have tufts of grass in it; and then, when they had gone a little farther, there were beautiful patches of anemones, and hyacinths, and jonquils, and crown imperials, and they stopped 180 to gather them; and they got among some trees, and then, as they had nothing to guide them but the shadows, and these went all sorts of ways, they lost a great deal of time, and the trees became of taller growth; but they still ran on and on till they got into a thick forest where it was quite dark, and here Mopsa began to cry, for she was tired.

"If I could only begin to be a queen," she said to Jack, "I could go wherever I pleased. I am not a fairy, and yet I am not a proper queen. Oh, what shall I do? I cannot go any farther."

So Jack gave her some of the seeds of the melon, though it was so dark that he could scarcely find the way to her mouth, and then he took some himself, and they both felt that they were rested, and Jack comforted Mopsa.

"If you are not a queen yet," he said, "you will be by to-morrow morning; for when our shadows danced on before us yours was so very 181 nearly the same height as mine, that I could hardly see any difference."

When they reached the end of that great forest, and found themselves out in all sorts of moonlight, the first thing they did was to laugh,—the shadows looked so odd, sticking out in every direction; and the next thing they did was to stand back to back, and put their heels together, and touch their heads together, to see by the shadow which was the taller; and Jack was still the least bit in the world taller than Mopsa; so they knew she was not a queen yet, and they ate some more melon-seeds, and began to climb up the mountain.

They climbed till the trees of the forest looked no bigger than gooseberry bushes, and then they climbed till the whole forest looked only like a patch of moss; and then, when they got a little higher, they saw the wonderful river, a long way off, and the snow glittering on the peaks overhead; and while they were looking and wondering how they should find a pass, the moons 182 all went down, one after the other, and, if Mopsa had not found some glowworms, they would have been quite in the dark again. However, she took a dozen of them, and put them round Jack's ankles, so that when he walked he could see where he was going; and he found a little sheep-path, and she followed him.

Now they had noticed during the night how many shooting-stars kept darting about from time to time, and at last one shot close by them, and fell in the soft moss on before. There it lay shining; and Jack, though he began to feel very tired again, made haste to it, for he wanted to see what it was like.

It was not what you would have supposed. It was soft and round, and about the color of a ripe apricot; it was covered with fur, and in fact it was evidently alive, and had curled itself up into a round ball.

"The dear little thing!" said Jack, as he held it in his hand, and showed it to Mopsa; "how its heart beats. Is it frightened?"

"Who are you?" said Mopsa to the thing. "What is your name?"

The little creature made a sound that seemed like "Wisp."

"Uncurl yourself, Wisp," said Mopsa. "Jack and I want to look at you."

So Wisp unfolded himself, and showed two little black eyes, and spread out two long filmy wings. He was like a most beautiful bat, and the light he shed out illuminated their faces.

"It is only one of the air fairies," said Mopsa. "Pretty creature! It never did any harm, and would like to do us good if it knew how, for it knows that I shall be a queen very soon. Wisp, if you like, you may go and tell your friends and relations that we want to cross over the mountains, and if they can they may help us."

Upon this Wisp spread out his wings, and shot off again; and Jack's feet were so tired that he sat down, and pulled off one of his shoes, for he thought there was a stone in it. So he set the little red jar beside him, and 184 quite forgot what the stone-woman had said, but went on shaking his shoe, and buckling it, and admiring the glowworms round his ankle, till Mopsa said, "Darling Jack, I am so dreadfully tired! Give me some more melon-seeds." Then he lifted up the jar, and thought it felt very heavy; and when he put in his hand, jar, and melon, and seeds were all turned to stone together.

They were both very sorry, and they sat still for a minute or two, for they were much too tired to stir; and then shooting-stars began to appear in all directions. The fairy bat had told his friends and relations, and they were coming. One fell at Mopsa's feet, another in her lap; more, more, all about, behind, before, and over them. And they spread out long filmy wings, some of them a yard long, till Jack and Mopsa seemed to be enclosed in a perfect network of the rays of shooting-stars, and they were both a good deal frightened. Fifty or sixty shooting-stars, 185 with black eyes that could stare, were enough, they thought, to frighten anybody.

"If we had anything to sit upon," said Mopsa, "they could carry us over the pass." She had no sooner spoken than the largest of the bats bit off one of his own long wings, and laid it at Mopsa's feet. It did not seem to matter much to him that he had parted with it, for he shot out another wing directly, just as a comet shoots out a ray of light sometimes, when it approaches the sun.

Mopsa thanked the shooting fairy, and, taking the wing, began to stretch it, till it was large enough for her and Jack to sit upon. Then all the shooting fairies came round it, took its edges in their mouths, and began to fly away with it over the mountains. They went slowly, for Jack and Mopsa were heavy, and they flew very low, resting now and then; but in the course of time they carried the wing over the pass, and halfway down the other side. Then the sun came up; and the moment he appeared all their lovely 186 apricot-colored light was gone, and they only looked like common bats, such as you can see every evening.

They set down Jack and Mopsa, folded up their long wings, and hung down their heads.

Mopsa thanked them, and said they had been useful; but still they looked ashamed, and crept into little corners and crevices of the rock, to hide.

CHAPTER XIV. REEDS AND RUSHES.

'Tis merry, 'tis merry in Fairyland, Where Fairy birds are singing; When the court doth sit by the monarch's side, With bit and bridle ringing.
Walter Scott.

There were many fruit-trees on that slope of the mountain, and Jack and Mopsa, as they came down, gathered some fruit for breakfast, and did not feel very tired, for the long ride on the wing had rested them.

They could not see the plain, for a slight blue mist hung over it; but the sun was hot already, and as they came down they saw a beautiful bed of high reeds, and thought they would sit awhile and rest in it. A rill of clear water ran beside the bed, so when they had reached it they sat down, and began to consider what they should do next.

"Jack," said Mopsa, "did you see anything particular as you came down with the shooting-stars?"

"No, I saw nothing so interesting as they were," answered Jack. "I was looking at them and watching how they squeaked to one another, and how they had little hooks in their wings, with which they held the large wing that we sat on."

"But I saw something," said Mopsa. "Just as the sun rose I looked down, and in the loveliest garden I ever saw, and all among trees and woods, I saw a most beautiful castle. O, Jack! I am sure that castle is the place I am to live in, and now we have nothing to do but to find it. I shall soon be a queen, and there I shall reign."

"Then I shall be king there," said Jack; "shall I?"

"Yes, if you can," answered Mopsa. "Of course, whatever you can do you may do. And, Jack, this is a much better fairy country than either the stony land or the other that we first came to, for this castle is a real place! It will not melt away. There the people can work, they know how to love each other: common fairies cannot do that, I know. They can laugh and cry, and I shall teach them several things that they do not know yet. Oh! do let us make haste and find the castle."

So they arose; but they turned the wrong way, and by mistake walked farther and farther in among the reeds, whose feathery heads puffed into Mopsa's face, and Jack's coat was all covered with the fluffy seed.

"This is very odd," said Jack. "I thought this was only a small bed of reeds when we stepped into it; but really we must have walked a mile already."

But they walked on and on, till Mopsa grew quite faint, and her sweet face became very pale, for she knew that the beds of reeds were spreading faster than they walked, and then they shot up so high that it was impossible to see over their heads; so at last Jack and Mopsa were so tired that they sat down, and Mopsa began to cry.

However, Jack was the braver of the two this time, and he comforted Mopsa, and told her that she was nearly a queen, and would never reach her castle by sitting still. So she got up and took his hand, and he went on before, parting the reeds and pulling her after him, till all on a sudden they heard the sweetest sound in the world; it was like a bell, and it sounded again and again.

It was the castle clock, and it was striking twelve at noon.

As it finished striking they came out at the farther edge of the great bed of reeds, and there was the castle straight before them,—a beautiful castle, standing on the slope of a hill. The grass all about it was covered with beautiful flowers; two of the taller turrets were overgrown with ivy, and a flag was flying on a staff; but everything 191 was so silent and lonely that it made one sad to look on. As Jack and Mopsa drew near they trod as gently as they could, and did not say a word.

All the windows were shut, but there was a great door in the centre of the building, and they went towards it, hand in hand.

What a beautiful hall! The great door stood wide open, and they could see what a delightful place this must be to live in: it was paved with squares of blue and white marble, and here and there carpets were spread, with chairs and tables upon them. They looked and saw a great dome overhead, filled with windows of colored glass, and they cast down blue and golden and rosy reflections.

"There is my home that I shall live in," said Mopsa; and she came close to the door, and they both looked in, till at last she let go of Jack's hand, and stepped over the threshold.

The bell in the tower sounded again more sweetly than ever, and the instant Mopsa was 192 inside there came from behind the fluted columns, which rose up on every side, the brown doe, followed by troops of deer and fawns!

"Mopsa! Mopsa!" cried Jack, "come away! come back!" But Mopsa was too much astonished to stir, and something seemed to hold Jack from following; but he looked and looked, till, as the brown doe advanced, the door of the castle closed,—Mopsa was shut in, and Jack was left outside.

So Mopsa had come straight to the place she thought she had ran away from.

"But I am determined to get her away from those creatures," thought Jack; "she does not want to reign over deer." And he began to look about him, hoping to get in. It was of no use: all the windows in that front of the castle were high, and when he tried to go round, he came to a high wall with battlements. Against some parts of this wall the ivy grew, and looked as if it might have grown there for ages; its stems were thicker than his waist, and its branches 193 were spread over the surface like network; so by means of them he hoped to climb to the top.

He immediately began to try. Oh, how high the wall was! First he came to several sparrows' nests, and very much frightened the sparrows were; then he reached starlings' nests, and very angry the starlings were; but at last, just under the coping, he came to jackdaws' nests, and these birds were very friendly, and pointed out to him the best little holes for him to put his feet into. At last he reached the top, and found to his delight that the wall was three feet thick, and he could walk upon it quite comfortably, and look down into a lovely garden, where all the trees were in blossom, and creepers tossed their long tendrils from tree to tree, covered with puffs of yellow, or bells of white, or bunches and knots of blue or rosy bloom.

He could look down into the beautiful empty rooms of the castle, and he walked cautiously on the wall till he came to the west front, and reached a little casement window that had latticed panes. 194 Jack peeped in; nobody was there. He took his knife, and cut away a little bit of lead to let out the pane, and it fell with such a crash on the pavement below that he wondered it did not bring the deer over to look at what he was about. Nobody came.

He put in his hand and opened the latchet, and with very little trouble got down into the room. Still nobody was to be seen. He thought that the room, years ago, might have been a fairies' school-room, for it was strewn with books, slates, and all sorts of copybooks. A fine soft dust had settled down over everything,—pens, papers, and all. Jack opened a copybook: its pages were headed with maxims, just as ours are, which proved that these fairies must have been superior to such as he had hitherto come among. Jack read some of them:—

> Turn your back on the light, and you'll follow a shadow. The deaf queen Fate has dumb courtiers. If the hound is your foe, don't sleep in his kennel. That that is, is.

And so on; but nobody came, and no sound was heard, so he opened the door, and found himself in a long and most splendid gallery, all hung with pictures, and spread with a most beautiful carpet, which was as soft and white as a piece of wool, and wrought with a beautiful device. This was the letter M, with a crown and sceptre, and underneath a beautiful little boat, exactly like the one in which he had come up the river. Jack felt sure that this carpet had been made for Mopsa, and he went along the gallery upon it till he reached a grand staircase of oak that was almost black with age, and he stole gently down it, for he began to feel rather shy, more especially as he could now see the great hall under the dome, and that it had a beautiful lady in it, and many other people, but no deer at all.

These fairy people were something like the one-foot-one fairies, but much larger and more like children; and they had very gentle, happy faces, and seemed to be extremely glad and gay. 196 But seated on a couch, where lovely painted windows threw down all sorts of rainbow colors on her, was a beautiful fairy lady, as large as a woman. She had Mopsa in her arms, and was looking down upon her with eyes full of love, while at her side stood a boy, who was exactly and precisely like Jack himself. He had rather long light hair and gray eyes, and a velvet jacket. That was all Jack could see at first, but as he drew nearer the boy turned, and then Jack felt as if he was looking at himself in the glass.

Mopsa had been very tired, and now she was fast asleep, with her head on that lady's shoulder. The boy kept looking at her, and he seemed very happy indeed; so did the lady, and she presently told him to bring Jack something to eat.

It was rather a curious speech that she made to him; it was this:—

"Jack, bring Jack some breakfast."

"What!" thought Jack to himself, "has he got a face like mine, and a name like mine too?"

So that other Jack went away, and presently came back with a golden plate full of nice things to eat.

"I know you don't like me," he said, as he came up to Jack with the plate.

"Not like him?" repeated the lady; "and pray what reason have you for not liking my royal nephew?"

"O dame!" exclaimed the boy, and laughed.

The lady, on hearing this, turned pale, for she perceived that she herself had mistaken the one for the other.

"I see you know how to laugh," said the real Jack. "You are wiser people than those whom I went to first; but the reason I don't like you is, that you are so exactly like me."

"I am not!" exclaimed the boy. "Only hear him, dame! You mean, I suppose, that you are so exactly like me. I am sure I don't know what you mean by it."

"Nor I either," replied Jack, almost in a passion.

"It couldn't be helped, of course," said the other Jack.

"Hush! hush!" said the fairy woman; "don't wake our dear little Queen. Was it you, my royal nephew, who spoke last?"

"Yes, dame," answered the boy, and again he offered the plate; but Jack was swelling with indignation, and he gave the plate a push with his elbow, which scattered the fruit and bread on the ground.

"I won't eat it," he said; but when the other Jack went and picked it up again, and said, "Oh, yes, do, old fellow; it's not my fault, you know," he began to consider that it was no use being cross in Fairyland; so he forgave his double, and had just finished his breakfast when Mopsa woke.

CHAPTER XV. THE QUEEN'S WAND.

One, two, three, four; one, two, three, four; 'Tis still one, two, three, four. Mellow and silvery are the tones, But I wish the bells were more.

Southey.

Mopsa woke: she was rather too big to be nursed, for she was the size of Jack, and looked like a sweet little girl of ten years, but she did not always behave like one; sometimes she spoke as wisely as a grown-up woman, and sometimes she changed again and seemed like a child.

Mopsa lifted up her head and pushed back her long hair: her coronet had fallen off while she was in the bed of reeds; and she said to the beautiful dame,—

"I am a queen now."

"Yes, my sweet Queen," answered the lady, "I know you are."

"And you promise that you will be kind to me till I grow up," said Mopsa, "and love me, and teach me how to reign?"

"Yes," repeated the lady; "and I will love you too, just as if you were a mortal and I your mother."

"For I am only ten years old yet," said Mopsa, "and the throne is too big for me to sit upon; but I am a queen." And then she paused, and said, "Is it three o'clock?"

As she spoke, the sweet, clear bell of the castle sounded three times, and then chimes began to play: they played such a joyous tune that it made everybody sing. The dame sang, the crowd of fairies sang, the boy who was Jack's double sang, and Mopsa sang,—only Jack was silent,—and this was the song:—

The prince shall to the chase again, The dame has got her face again, The king shall have his place again Aneath the fairy dome.

201 And all the knights shall woo again, And all the doves shall coo again, And all the dreams come true again, And Jack shall go home.

"We shall see about that!" thought Jack to himself. And Mopsa, while she sang those last words, burst into tears, which Jack did not like to see; but all the fairies were so very glad, so joyous, and so delighted with her for having come to be their queen, that after a while she dried her eyes, and said to the wrong boy,—

"Jack, when I pulled the lining out of your pocket-book there was a silver fourpence in it."

"Yes," said the real Jack, "and here it is."

"Is it real money?" asked Mopsa. "Are you sure you brought it with you all the way from your own country?"

"Yes," said Jack, "quite sure."

"Then, dear Jack," answered Mopsa, "will you give it to me?"

"I will," said Jack, "if you will send this boy away."

"How can I?" answered Mopsa, surprised. "Don't you know what happened when the door closed? Has nobody told you?"

"I did not see any one after I got into the place," said Jack. "There was no one to tell anything,—not even a fawn, nor the brown doe. I have only seen down here these fairy people, and this boy, and this lady."

"The lady is the brown doe," answered Mopsa; "and this boy and the fairies were the fawns." Jack was so astonished at this that he stared at the lady and the boy and the fairies with all his might.

"The sun came shining in as I stepped inside," said Mopsa, "and a long beam fell down from the fairy dome across my feet. Do you remember what the apple-woman told us,—how it was reported that the brown doe and her nation had a queen whom they shut up, and never let the sun shine on her? That was not a kind or true report, and yet it came from something that really happened."

"Yes, I remember," said Jack; "and if the sun did shine they were all to be turned into deer."

"I dare not tell you all that story yet," said Mopsa; "but, Jack, as the brown doe and all the fawns came up to greet me, and passed by turns into the sunbeam, they took their own forms, every one of them, because the spell was broken. They were to remain in the disguise of deer till a queen of alien birth should come to them against her will. I am a queen of alien birth, and did not I come against my will?"

"Yes, to be sure," answered Jack. "We thought all the time that we were running away."

"If ever you come to Fairyland again," observed Mopsa, "you can save yourself the trouble of trying to run away from the old mother."

"I shall not 'come,'" answered Jack, "because I shall not go,—not for a long while, at least. 204 But the boy,—I want to know why this boy turned into another ME?"

"Because he is the heir, of course," answered Mopsa.

"But I don't see that this is any reason at all," said Jack.

Mopsa laughed. "That's because you don't know how to argue," she replied. "Why, the thing is as plain as possible."

"It may be plain to you," persisted Jack, "but it's no reason."

"No reason!" repeated Mopsa, "no reason! when I like you the best of anything in the world, and when I am come here to be queen? Of course, when the spell was broken he took exactly your form on that account; and very right too."

"But why?" asked Jack.

Mopsa, however, was like other fairies in this respect,—that she knew all about Old Mother Fate, but not about causes and reasons. She believed, as we do in this world, that

> That that is, is;

but the fairies go further than this; they say:—

> That that is, is; and when it is, that is the reason that it is.

This sounds like nonsense to us, but it is all right to them.

So Mopsa, thinking she had explained everything, said again,—

"And, dear Jack, will you give the silver fourpence to me?"

Jack took it out; and she got down from the dame's knee and took it in the palm of her hand, laying the other palm upon it.

"It will be very hot," observed the dame.

"But it will not burn me so as really to hurt, if I am a real queen," said Mopsa.

Presently she began to look as if something gave her pain.

"Oh, it's so hot!" she said to the other Jack; "so very hot!"

"Never mind, sweet Queen," he answered; "it will not hurt you long. Remember my poor uncle and all his knights."

Mopsa still held the little silver coin; but Jack saw that it hurt her, for two bright tears fell from her eyes; and in another moment he saw that it was actually melted, for it fell in glittering drops from Mopsa's hand to the marble floor, and there it lay as soft as quicksilver.

"Pick it up," said Mopsa to the other Jack; and he instantly did so, and laid it in her hand again; and she began gently to roll it backwards and forwards between her palms till she had rolled it into a very slender rod, two feet long, and not nearly so thick as a pin; but it did not bend, and it shone so brightly that you could hardly look at it.

Then she held it out towards the real Jack, and said, "Give this a name."

"I think it is a——" began the other Jack; but the dame suddenly stopped him. "Silence, sire! Don't you know that what it is first called that it will be?"

Jack hesitated; he thought if Mopsa was a queen the thing ought to be a sceptre; but it certainly was not at all like a sceptre.

"That thing is a wand," said he.

"You are a wand," said Mopsa, speaking to the silver stick, which was glittering now in a sunbeam almost as if it were a beam of light itself. Then she spoke again to Jack:

"Tell me, Jack, what can I do with a wand?"

Again the boy-king began to speak, and the dame stopped him, and again Jack considered. He had heard a great deal in his own country about fairy wands, but he could not remember that the fairies had done anything particular with them, so he gave what he thought was true, but what seemed to him a very stupid answer:

"You can make it point to anything that you please."

The moment he had said this, shouts of ecstasy filled the hall, and all the fairies clapped their hands with such hurrahs of delight that he blushed for joy.

The dame also looked truly glad, and as for the other Jack, he actually turned head over heels, just as Jack had often done himself on his father's lawn.

Jack had merely meant that Mopsa could point with the wand to anything that she saw; but he was presently told that what he had meant was nothing, and that his words were everything.

"I can make it point now," said Mopsa, "and it will point aright to anything I please, whether I know where the thing is or not."

Again the hall was filled with those cries of joy, and the sweet, child-like fairies congratulated each other with "The Queen has got a wand,—a wand! and she can make it point wherever she pleases!"

Then Mopsa rose and walked towards the beautiful staircase, the dame and all the fairies following. Jack was going too, but the other Jack held him.

"Where is Mopsa going? and why am I not to follow?" inquired Jack.

"They are going to put on her robes, of course," answered the other Jack.

"I am so tired of always hearing you say 'of course,'" answered Jack; "and I wonder how it is that you always seem to know what is going to be done without being told. However, I suppose you can't help being odd people."

The boy-king did not make a direct answer; he only said, "I like you very much, though you don't like me."

"Why do you like me?" asked Jack.

So he opened his eyes wide with surprise: "Most boys say Sire to me," he observed; "at least they used to do when there were any boys here. However, that does not signify. Why, of course I like you, because I am so tired of being always a fawn, and you brought Mopsa to break the spell. You cannot think how disagreeable it is to have no hands, and to be all covered with hair. Now look at my hands; I can move them and turn them everywhere, even over my head 210 if I like. Hoofs are good for nothing in comparison; and we could not talk."

"Do tell me about it," said Jack. "How did you become fawns?"

"I dare not tell you," said the boy; "and listen!—I hear Mopsa."

Jack looked, and certainly Mopsa was coming, but very strangely, he thought. Mopsa, like all other fairies, was afraid to whisper a spell with her eyes open; so a handkerchief was tied across them, and as she came on she felt her way, holding by the banisters with one hand, and with the other, between her finger and thumb, holding out the silver wand. She felt with her foot for the edge of the first stair; and Jack heard her say, "I am much older,—ah! so much older, now I have got my wand. I can feel sorrow too, and their sorrow weighs down my heart."

Mopsa was dressed superbly in a white satin gown, with a long, long train of crimson velvet which was glittering with diamonds; it reached almost from one end of the great gallery to the 211 other, and had hundreds of fairies to hold it and keep it in its place. But in her hair were no jewels, only a little crown made of daisies, and on her shoulders her robe was fastened with the little golden image of a boat. These things were to show the land she had come from and the vessel she had come in.

So she came slowly, slowly down stairs blindfold, and muttering to her wand all the time:
    Though the sun shine brightly, Wand, wand, guide rightly.

So she felt her way down to the great hall. There the wand turned half round in the hall toward the great door, and she and Jack and the other Jack came out into the lawn in front with all the followers and trainbearers; only the dame remained behind.

Jack noticed now for the first time that, with the one exception of the boy-king, all these fairies were lady-fairies; he also observed that Mopsa, after the manner of fairy queens, though she moved slowly and blindfold, was beginning to 212 tell a story. This time it did not make him feel sleepy. It did not begin at the beginning: their stories never do.

These are the first words he heard, for she spoke softly and very low, while he walked at her right hand, and the other Jack on her left:

"And so now I have no wings. But my thoughts can go up (Jovinian and Roxaletta could not think). My thoughts are instead of wings; but they have dropped with me now, as a lark among the clods of the valley. Wand, do you bend? Yes, I am following, wand.

"And after that the bird said, 'I will come when you call me.' I never have seen her moving overhead; perhaps she is out of sight. Flocks of birds hover over the world, and watch it high up where the air is thin. There are zones, but those in the lowest zone are far out of sight.

"I have not been up there. I have no wings.

"Over the highest of the birds is the place 213 where angels float and gather the children's souls as they are set free.

"And so that woman told me,—(Wand, you bend again, and I will turn at your bending),—that woman told me how it was: for when the new king was born, a black fairy with a smiling face came and sat within the doorway. She had a spindle, and would always spin. She wanted to teach them how to spin, but they did not like her, and they loved to do nothing at all. So they turned her out.

"But after her came a brown fairy, with a grave face, and she sat on the black fairy's stool and gave them much counsel. They liked that still less; so they got spindles and spun, for they said, 'She will go now, and we shall have the black fairy again.' When she did not go they turned her out also, and after her came a white fairy, and sat in the same seat. She did nothing at all, and she said nothing at all; but she had a sorrowful face, and she looked up. So they were displeased. They turned her out also; and 214 she went and sat by the edge of the lake with her two sisters.

"And everything prospered over all the land; till, after shearing-time, the shepherds, because the king was a child, came to his uncle and said, 'Sir, what shall we do with the old wool, for the new fleeces are in the bales, and there is no storehouse to put them in?' So he said, 'Throw them into the lake.'

"And while they threw them in, a great flock of finches flew to them, and said, 'Give us some of the wool that you do not want; we should be glad of it to build our nests with.'

"They answered, 'Go and gather for yourselves; there is wool on every thorn.'

"Then the black fairy said, 'They shall be forgiven this time, because the birds should pick wool for themselves.'

"So the finches flew away.

"Then the harvest was over, and the reapers came and said to the child-king's uncle, 'Sir, what shall we do with the new wheat, for the 215 old is not half eaten yet, and there is no room in the granaries?'

"He said, 'Throw that into the lake also.'

"While they were throwing it in, there came a great flight of the wood fairies, fairies of passage from over the sea. They were in the form of pigeons, and they alighted and prayed them, 'O, cousins! we are faint with our long flight; give us some of that corn which you do not want, that we may peck it and be refreshed.'

"But they said, 'You may rest on our land, but our corn is our own. Rest awhile, and go and get food in your own fields.'

"Then the brown fairy said, 'They may be forgiven this once, but yet it is a great unkindness.'

"And as they were going to pour in the last sackful, there passed a poor mortal beggar, who had strayed in from the men and women's world, and she said, 'Pray give me some of that wheat, O fairy people! for I am hungry. I have lost my way, and there is no money to be earned here. Give me some of that wheat, that I may bake cakes, lest I and my baby should starve.'

"And they said, 'What is starve? We never heard that word before, and we cannot wait while you explain it to us.'

"So they poured it all into the lake; and then the white fairy said, 'This cannot be forgiven them'; and she covered her face with her hands and wept. Then the black fairy rose and drove them all before her,—the prince, with his chief shepherd and his reapers, his courtiers and his knights; she drove them into the great bed of reeds, and no one has ever set eyes on them since. Then the brown fairy went into the palace where the king's aunt sat, with all her ladies and her maids about her, and with the child-king on her knee.

"It was a very gloomy day.

"She stood in the middle of the hall, and said, 'Oh, you cold-hearted and most unkind! my spell is upon you, and the first ray of sunshine shall bring it down. Lose your present forms, and be of a more gentle and innocent race, till a queen of alien birth shall come to reign over you against her will.'

"As she spoke they crept into corners, and covered the dame's head with a veil. And all that day it was dark and gloomy, and nothing happened, and all the next day it rained and rained; and they thrust the dame into a dark closet, and kept her there for a whole month, and still not a ray of sunshine came to do them any damage; but the dame faded and faded in the dark, and at last they said, 'She must come out, or she will die; and we do not believe the sun will ever shine in our country any more.' So they let the poor dame come out; and lo! as she crept slowly forth under the dome, a piercing ray of sunlight darted down upon her head, and in an instant they were all changed into deer, and the child-king too.

"They are gentle now, and kind; but where is the prince? where are the fairy knights and the fairy men?

"Wand! why do you turn?"

Now while Mopsa told her story the wand continued to bend, and Mopsa, following, was slowly approaching the foot of a great precipice, which rose sheer up for more than a hundred feet. The crowd that followed looked dismayed at this: they thought the wand must be wrong; or even if it was right, they could not climb a precipice.

But still Mopsa walked on blindfold, and the wand pointed at the rock till it touched it, and she said, "Who is stopping me?"

They told her, and she called to some of her ladies to untie the handkerchief. Then Mopsa looked at the rock, and so did the two Jacks. There was nothing to be seen but a very tiny hole. The boy-king thought it led to a bees' nest, and Jack thought it was a keyhole, for he noticed in the rock a slight crack which took the shape of an arched door.

Mopsa looked earnestly at the hole. "It may be a keyhole," she said, "but there is no key."

CHAPTER XVI. FAILURE.

We are much bound to them that do succeed; But, in a more pathetic sense, are bound To such as fail. They all our loss expound; They comfort us for work that will not speed, And life—itself a failure. Ay, his deed, Sweetest in story, who the dusk profound Of Hades flooded with entrancing sound, Music's own tears, was failure. Doth it read Therefore the worse? Ah, no! so much to dare, He fronts the regnant Darkness on its throne.— So much to do; impetuous even there, He pours out love's disconsolate sweet moan— He wins; but few for that his deed recall:
Its power is in the look which costs him all.

At this moment Jack observed that a strange woman was standing among them, and that the trainbearing fairies fell back, as if they were afraid of her. As no one spoke, he did, and said, "Good-morning!"

"Good-afternoon!" she answered, correcting him. "I am the black fairy. Work is a fine thing. Most people in your country can work."

"Yes," said Jack.

"There are two spades," continued the fairy woman, "one for you, and one for your double."

Jack took one of the spades,—it was small, and was made of silver; but the other Jack said with scorn,—

"I shall be a king when I am old enough, and must I dig like a clown?"

"As you please," said the black fairy, and walked away.

Then they all observed that a brown woman was standing there; and she stepped up and whispered in the boy-king's ear. As he listened his sullen face became good tempered, and at last he said, in a gentle tone, "Jack, I'm quite ready to begin if you are."

"But where are we to dig?" asked Jack.

"There," said a white fairy, stepping up and setting her foot on the grass just under the little hole. "Dig down as deep as you can."

So Mopsa and the crowd stood back, and the two boys began to dig; and greatly they enjoyed it, for people can dig so fast in Fairyland.

Very soon the hole was so deep that they had to jump into it, because they could not reach the bottom with their spades. "This is very jolly indeed," said Jack, when they had dug so much deeper that they could only see out of the hole by standing on tiptoe.

"Go on," said the white fairy; so they dug till they came to a flat stone, and then she said, "Now you can stamp. Stamp on the stone, and don't be afraid." So the two Jacks began to stamp, and in such a little time that she had only half turned her head round, the flat stone gave way, for there was a hollow underneath it, and down went the boys, and utterly disappeared.

Then, while Mopsa and the crowd silently looked on, the white fairy lightly pushed the clods of earth towards the hole with the side of her foot, and in a very few minutes the hole was filled in, and that so completely and so neatly, that when she had spread the turf on it, and given it a pat with her foot, you could not have told where it had been. Mopsa said not a word, for no fairy ever interferes with a stronger fairy; but she looked on earnestly, and when the white stranger smiled she was satisfied.

Then the white stranger walked away, and Mopsa and the fairies sat down on a bank under some splendid cedar-trees. The beautiful castle looked fairer than ever in the afternoon sunshine; a lovely waterfall tumbled with a tinkling noise near at hand, and the bank was covered with beautiful wild flowers.

They sat for a long while, and no one spoke: what they were thinking of is not known, but sweet Mopsa often sighed.

At last a noise,—a very, very slight noise, as of the footsteps of people running,—was heard inside the rock, and then a little quivering was 223 seen in the wand. It quivered more and more as the sound increased. At last that which had looked like a door began to shake as if some one was pushing it from within. Then a noise was distinctly heard as of a key turning in the hole, and out burst the two Jacks, shouting for joy, and a whole troop of knights and squires and serving-men came rushing wildly forth behind them.

Oh, the joy of that meeting! who shall describe it? Fairies by dozens came up to kiss the boy-king's hand, and Jack shook hands with every one that could reach him. Then Mopsa proceeded to the castle between the two Jacks, and the king's aunt came out to meet them, and welcomed her husband with tears of joy; for these fairies could laugh and cry when they pleased, and they naturally considered this a great proof of superiority.

After this a splendid feast was served under the great dome. The other fairy feasts that Jack had seen were nothing to it. The prince and his dame 224 sat at one board, but Mopsa sat at the head of the great table, with the two Jacks, one on each side of her.

Mopsa was not happy, Jack was sure of that, for she often sighed; and he thought this strange. But he did not ask her any questions, and he, with the boy-king, related their adventures to her: how, when the stone gave way, they tumbled in and rolled down a sloping bank till they found themselves at the entrance of a beautiful cave, which was all lighted up with torches, and glittering with stars and crystals of all the colors in the world. There was a table spread with what looked like a splendid luncheon in this great cave, and chairs were set round, but Jack and the boy-king felt no inclination to eat anything, though they were hungry, for a whole nation of ants were creeping up the honey-pots. There were snails walking about over the table-cloth, and toads peeping out of some of the dishes.

So they turned away, and, looking for some other door to lead them farther in, they at last 225 found a very small one,—so small that only one of them could pass through at a time.

They did not tell Mopsa all that had occurred on this occasion. It was thus:

The boy-king said, "I shall go in first, of course, because of my rank."

"Very well," said Jack, "I don't mind. I shall say to myself that you've gone in first to find the way for me, because you're my double. Besides, now I think of it, our Queen always goes last in a procession; so it's grand to go last. Pass in, Jack."

"No," answered the other Jack; "now you have said that I will not. You may go first."

So they began to quarrel and argue about this, and it is impossible to say how long they would have gone on if they had not begun to hear a terrible and mournful sort of moaning and groaning, which frightened them both and instantly made them friends. They took tight hold of one another's hand, and again there came by a loud sighing, and a noise of all sorts of lamentation, 226 and it seemed to reach them through the little door.

Each of the boys would now have been very glad to go back, but neither liked to speak. At last Jack thought anything would be less terrible than listening to those dismal moans, so he suddenly dashed through the door, and the other Jack followed.

There was nothing terrible to be seen. They found themselves in a place like an immensely long stable; but it was nearly dark, and when their eyes got used to the dimness, they saw that it was strewed with quantities of fresh hay, from which curious things like sticks stuck up in all directions. What were they?

"They are dry branches of trees," said the boy-king.

"They are table-legs turned upside down," said Jack: but then the other Jack suddenly perceived the real nature of the thing, and he shouted out, "No; they are antlers!"

The moment he said this the moaning ceased, 227 hundreds of beautiful antlered heads were lifted up, and the two boys stood before a splendid herd of stags; but they had had hardly time to be sure of this when the beautiful multitude rose and fled away into the darkness, leaving the two boys to follow as well as they could.

They were sure they ought to run after the herd, and they ran and ran, but they soon lost sight of it, though they heard far on in front what seemed at first like a pattering of deer's feet, but the sound changed from time to time. It became heavier and louder, and then the clattering ceased, and it was evidently the tramping of a great crowd of men. At last they heard words, very glad and thankful words; people were crying to one another to make haste, lest the spell should come upon them again. Then the two Jacks, still running, came into a grand hall, which was quite full of knights and all sorts of fairy men, and there was the boy-king's uncle, but he looked very pale. "Unlock the door!" they cried. "We shall not be safe till we see 228 our new Queen. Unlock the door; we see light coming through the keyhole."

The two Jacks came on to the front, and felt and shook the door. At last the boy-king saw a little golden key glittering on the floor, just where the one narrow sunbeam fell that came through the keyhole; so he snatched it up. It fitted, and out they all came, as you have been told.

When they had done relating their adventures, the new Queen's health was drunk. And then they drank the health of the boy-king, who stood up to return thanks, and, as is the fashion there, he sang a song. Jack thought it the most ridiculous song he had ever heard; but as everybody else looked extremely grave, he tried to be grave too. It was about Cock-Robin and Jenny Wren, how they made a wedding feast, and how the wren said she should wear her brown gown, and the old dog brought a bone to the feast.

"He had brought them," he said, "some meat on a bone: They were welcome to pick it or leave it alone."

The fairies were very attentive to this song; 229 they seemed, if one may judge by their looks, to think it was rather a serious one. Then they drank Jack's health, and afterwards looked at him as if they expected him to sing too; but as he did not begin, he presently heard them whispering, and one asking another, "Do you think he knows manners?"

So he thought he had better try what he could do, and he stood up and sang a song that he had often heard his nurse sing in the nursery at home.

One morning, oh! so early, my belovèd, my belovèd, All the birds were singing blithely, as if never they would cease; 'Twas a thrush sang in my garden, "Hear the story, hear the story!" And the lark sang, "Give us glory!" And the dove said, "Give us peace!"

Then I listened, oh! so early, my belovèd, my belovèd, To that murmur from the woodland of the dove, my dear, the dove; When the nightingale came after, "Give us fame to sweeten duty!"

When the wren sang, "Give us beauty!" She made answer, "Give us love!"

230 Sweet is spring, and sweet the morning, my belovèd, my belovèd; Now for us doth spring, doth morning, wait upon the year's increase, And my prayer goes up, "Oh, give us, crowned in youth with marriage glory, Give for all our life's dear story, Give us love, and give us peace!"

"A very good song too," said the dame, at the other end of the table; "only you made a mistake in the first verse. What the dove really said was, no doubt, 'Give us peas.' All kinds of doves and pigeons are very fond of peas."

"It isn't peas, though," said Jack. However, the court historian was sent for to write down the song, and he came with a quill pen, and wrote it down as the dame said it ought to be.

Now all this time Mopsa sat between the two Jacks, and she looked very mournful,—she hardly said a word.

When the feast was over, and everything had vanished, the musicians came in, for there was to be dancing; but while they were striking up, 231 the white fairy stepped in, and, coming up, whispered something in Jack's ear; but he could not hear what she said, so she repeated it more slowly, and still he could neither hear nor understand it.

Mopsa did not seem to like the white fairy; she leaned her face on her hand and sighed; but when she found that Jack could not hear the message, she said, "That is well. Cannot you let things alone for this one day?" The fairy then spoke to Mopsa, but she would not listen; she made a gesture of dislike and moved away. So then this strange fairy turned and went out again, but on the door-step she looked round, and beckoned to Jack to come to her. So he did; and then, as they two stood together outside, she made him understand what she had said. It was this:

"Her name was Jenny, her name was Jenny."

When Jack understood what she said he felt so sorrowful; he wondered why she had told him, and he longed to stay in that great place with 232 Queen Mopsa,—his own little Mopsa, whom he had carried in his pocket, and taken care of, and loved.

He walked up and down, up and down, outside, and his heart swelled and his eyes filled with tears. The bells had said he was to go home, and the fairy had told him how to go. Mopsa did not need him, she had so many people to take care of her; and then there was that boy, so exactly like himself that she would not miss him. Oh, how sorrowful it all was! Had he really come up the fairy river, and seen those strange countries, and run away with Mopsa over those dangerous mountains, only to bring her to the very place she wished to fly from, and there to leave her, knowing that she wanted him no more, and that she was quite content?

No; Jack felt that he could not do that. "I will stay," he said; "they cannot make me leave her. That would be too unkind."

As he spoke, he drew near to the great yawning door, and looked in. The fairy folk were singing inside; he could hear their pretty chirping voices, and see their beautiful faces, but he could not bear it, and he turned away.

The sun began to get low, and all the west was dyed with crimson. Jack dried his eyes, and, not liking to go in, took one turn more.

"I will go in," he said; "there is nothing to prevent me." He set his foot on the step of the door, and while he hesitated Mopsa came out to meet him.

"Jack," she said, in a sweet mournful tone of voice. But he could not make any answer; he only looked at her earnestly, because her lovely eyes were not looking at him, but far away towards the west.

"He lives there," she said, as if speaking to herself. "He will play there again, in his father's garden."

Then she brought her eyes down slowly from the rose-flush in the cloud, and looked at him and said, "Jack."

"Yes," said Jack; "I am here. What is it that you wish to say?"

She answered, "I am come to give you back your kiss."

So she stooped forward as she stood on the step, and kissed him, and her tears fell on his cheek.

"Farewell!" she said, and she turned and went up the steps and into the great hall; and while Jack gazed at her as she entered, and would fain have followed, but could not stir, the great doors closed together again, and he was left outside.

Then he knew, without having been told, that he should never enter them any more. He stood gazing at the castle; but it was still,—no more fairy music sounded.

How beautiful it looked in the evening sunshine, and how Jack cried!

THE QUEEN'S FAREWELL.

"She stooped forward as she stood on the step, and kissed him."—.

Suddenly he perceived that reeds were growing up between him and the great doors: the grass, which had all day grown about the steps, was getting taller; it had long spear-like leaves, it pushed up long pipes of green stem, and they whistled.

They were up to his ankles, they were presently up to his waist; soon they were as high as his head. He drew back that he might see over them; they sprang up faster as he retired, and again he went back. It seemed to him that the castle also receded; there was a long reach of these great reeds between it and him, and now they were growing behind also, and on all sides of him. He kept moving back and back: it was of no use, they sprang up and grew yet more tall, till very shortly the last glimpse of the fairy castle was hidden from his sorrowful eyes.

The sun was just touching the tops of the purple mountains when Jack lost sight of Mopsa's home; but he remembered how he had penetrated the bed of reeds in the morning, and he hoped to have the same good fortune again. So on and on he walked, pressing his way among them as well as he could, till the sun went down 236 behind the mountains, and the rosy sky turned gold color, and the gold began to burn itself away, and then all on a sudden he came to the edge of the reed-bed, and walked out upon a rising ground.

Jack ran up it, looking for the castle. He could not see it, so he climbed a far higher hill; still he could not see it. At last, after a toilsome ascent to the very top of the green mountain, he saw the castle lying so far, so very far off, that its peaks and its battlements were on the edge of the horizon, and the evening mist rose while he was gazing, so that all its outlines were lost, and very soon they seemed to mingle with the shapes of the hill and the forest, till they had utterly vanished away.

Then he threw himself down on the short grass. The words of the white fairy sounded in his ears, "Her name was Jenny"; and he burst into tears again, and decided to go home.

He looked up into the rosy sky, and held out his arms, and called, "Jenny! O Jenny! come."

In a minute or two he saw a little black mark overhead, a small speck, and it grew larger, and larger, and larger still, as it fell headlong down like a stone. In another instant he saw a red light and a green light, then he heard the winnowing noise of the bird's great wings, and she alighted at his feet, and said, "Here I am."

"I wish to go home," said Jack, hanging down his head and speaking in a low voice, for his heart was heavy because of his failure.

"That is well," answered the bird. She took Jack on her back, and in three minutes they were floating among the clouds.

As Jack's feet were lifted up from Fairyland he felt a little consoled. He began to have a curious feeling, as if this had all happened a good while ago, and then half the sorrow he had felt faded into wonder, and the feeling still grew upon him that these things had passed some great while since, so that he repeated to himself, "It was a long time ago."

Then he fell asleep, and did not dream at all, 238 nor know anything more till the bird woke him.

"Wake up now, Jack," she said; "we are at home."

"So soon!" said Jack, rubbing his eyes. "But it is evening; I thought it would be morning."

"Fairy time is always six hours in advance of your time," said the bird. "I see glowworms down in the hedge, and the moon is just rising."

They were falling so fast that Jack dared not look; but he saw the church, and the wood, and his father's house, which seemed to be starting up to meet him. In two seconds more the bird alighted, and he stepped down from her back into the deep grass of his father's meadow.

"Good-by!" she said; "make haste and run in, for the dews are falling"; and before he could ask her one question, or even thank her, she made a wide sweep over the grass, beat her magnificent wings, and soared away.

It was all very extraordinary, and Jack felt shy and ashamed; but he knew he must go 239 home, so he opened the little gate that led into the garden, and stole through the shrubbery, hoping that his footsteps would not be heard.

Then he came out on the lawn, where the flower-beds were, and he observed that the drawing-room window was open, so he came softly towards it and peeped in.

His father and mother were sitting there. Jack was delighted to see them, but he did not say a word, and he wondered whether they would be surprised at his having stayed away so long. The bird had said that they would not.

He drew a little nearer. His mother sat with her back to the open window, but a candle was burning, and she was reading aloud. Jack listened as she read, and knew that this was not in the least like anything that he had seen in Fairyland, nor the reading like anything that he had heard, and he began to forget the boy-king, and the apple-woman, and even his little Mopsa, more and more.

At last his father noticed him. He did not look 240 at all surprised, but just beckoned to him with his finger to come in. So Jack did, and got upon his father's knee, where he curled himself up comfortably, laid his head on his father's waistcoat, and wondered what he would think if he should be told about the fairies in somebody else's waistcoat pocket. He thought, besides, what a great thing a man was; he had never seen anything so large in Fairyland, nor so important; so, on the whole, he was glad he had come back, and felt very comfortable. Then his mother, turning over the leaf, lifted up her eyes and looked at Jack, but not as if she was in the least surprised, or more glad to see him than usual; but she smoothed the leaf with her hand, and began again to read, and this time it was about the Shepherd Lady:—

I.

Who pipes upon the long green hill, Where meadow grass is deep? The white lamb bleats but followeth on— Follow the clean white sheep. The dear white lady in yon high tower, She hearkeneth in her sleep.

241 All in long grass the piper stands, Goodly and grave is he; Outside the tower, at dawn of day, The notes of his pipe ring free. A thought from his heart doth reach to hers: "Come down, O lady! to me."

She lifts her head, she dons her gown: Ah! the lady is fair; She ties the girdle on her waist, And binds her flaxen hair, And down she stealeth, down and down, Down the turret stair.

Behold him! With the flock he wons Along yon grassy lea. "My shepherd lord, my shepherd love, What wilt thou, then, with me? My heart is gone out of my breast, And followeth on to thee."

242 II.

"The white lambs feed in tender grass: With them and thee to bide, How good it were," she saith at noon; "Albeit the meads are wide. Oh! well is me" she saith when day Draws on to eventide.

Hark! hark! the shepherd's voice. Oh, sweet! Her tears drop down like rain. "Take now this crook, my chosen, my fere And tend the flock full fain; Feed them, O lady, and lose not one, Till I shall come again."

Right soft her speech: "My will is thine, And my reward thy grace!" Gone are his footsteps over the hill, Withdrawn his goodly face; The mournful dusk begins to gather, The daylight wanes apace.

243 III.

On sunny slopes, ah! long the lady Feedeth her flock at noon; She leads them down to drink at eve Where the small rivulets croon. All night her locks are wet with dew, Her eyes outwatch the moon.

Over the hills her voice is heard, She sings when light doth wane: "My longing heart is full of love. When shall my loss be gain? My shepherd lord, I see him not, But he will come again."

When she had finished, Jack lifted his face and said, "Mamma!" Then she came to him and kissed him, and his father said, "I think it must be time this man of ours was in bed."

So he looked earnestly at them both, and as they still asked him no questions, he kissed and wished them good-night; and his mother said 244 there were some strawberries on the sideboard in the dining-room, and he might have them for his supper.

So he ran out into the hall, and was delighted to find all the house just as usual, and after he had looked about him he went into his own room, and said his prayers. Then he got into his little white bed, and comfortably fell asleep.

That's all.

Printed in Great Britain
by Amazon